UK
SUPERMARKET...
2014-2020

How it started, who's winning, and why

G. N. C. Parker

Plain Press Limited

For Sue

This paperback edition first published in Great Britain in 2017 by
Plain Press Limited
4b Church Street
Diss, Norfolk IP22 4DD

A catalogue record for this book is available from the British Library.

ISBN: 978-0-9957914-0-4

Contents

Preface 1

CHAPTER 1: SUMMARY 2

Topic 1: About the wars 2

Topic 2: About this book 6

Topic 3: Who this book is for 11

Topic 4: Predictions for 2020 15

Topic 5: Summary of secrets 22

Topic 6: Word usage & notes 24

CHAPTER 2: BACKGROUND 29

Topic 7: No bobbing corks 29

Topic 8: Acting on purpose 33

Topic 9: Illiad Case Study 39

Topic 10: Market data 42

Topic 11: Ops Mgmt: the 90s 45

Topic 12: Mktg Mgmt: the 90s 52

CHAPTER 3: SHOPPERS 58

Topic 13: Enter the dragon 58

Topic 14: Case Study: Mktg 60

Topic 15: Johnny British: 1995 64

Topic 16: Customers: 1995 71

Topic 17: The flip side: 1995 75

Topic 18: Aim for mood: 2015 79

Topic 19: Impulsion: 1996 82

CHAPTER 4: MARGINS 84

Topic 20: Whose profit? 84

Topic 21: Accounting talk 87

Topic 22: Margin magic 91

Topic 23: Margin secrets 95

Topic 24: Margin games 99

Topic 25: Push up sales? 102

Topic 26: Cut costs? 105

Topic 27: Swap FC with VC? 108

CHAPTER 5: FRAMEWORKS 111

Topic 28: Strategy 111

Topic 29: Decide on scope 115

Topic 30: Points of difference 119

Topic 31: Being disruptive 122

Topic 32: Using frameworks 126

Topic 33: Implementing: 1995 130

CHAPTER 6: SECRETS 132

Topic 34: Unpack the mantra 132

Topic 35: Why keep it small? 136

Topic 36: How to speed it up 140

Topic 37: Fast shopping: 1996 143

Topic 38: Arithmetic: 1996 .... *150*

Topic 39: Finding flow: 2015 .... *156*

Topic 40: Missing flow: 1996 .... *161*

Topic 41: The story so far *165*

CHAPTER 7: ISSUES *167*

Topic 42: Growing: 1995 .... *167*

Topic 43: Team building: 1996 .... *169*

Topic 44: Store brands: 1996 .... *172*

Topic 45: Suppliers: 1996 .... *180*

Topic 46: Long tail: 1996 .... *186*

Topic 47: EDLP vs Bogoff *189*

Topic 48: The public company *193*

Topic 49: Private firms: 1997 .... *200*

Topic 50: Stealth mode: 2014 .... *206*

CHAPTER 8: GROWTH *209*

Topic 51: Making space *209*

Topic 52: Gearing vs leverage *212*

Topic 53: Reverse gearing *219*

Topic 54: Penny or bun? *224*

CHAPTER 9: OPTIONS *231*

Topic 55: Future shocks: 2015 .... *231*

Topic 56: Hard or soft landing *235*

Topic 57: Match or tweak? *238*

Topic 58: Cramming *246*

Topic 59: Scoreboard: recap 249

Topic 60: Update: coverage 253

Acknowledgements 259

About the author 261

Index 262

Preface

AUTHOR G. N. C. PARKER describes a new kind of grocery war that the official experts have missed. The Big Four supermarkets are losing market share to a couple of up-start rivals (aka the 'German discounters') and they don't seem to know how to stop it.

The author says that there are at least 27 million shopping experts in the UK, one from each household. It's these shoppers who decide who wins the war.

For the first time ever we are shown why the up-starts are winning. It has nothing to do with 'buying power', 'cutting corners', or 'piling it high'. Nor does it have that much to do with online retail. The author knows that online retail is a threat to high street retailers, but he shows why grocery stores are different.

If you are a shopper or student you may enjoy this book and find it useful. But if you own or work in any type of retail firm, you may want to read it asap. The author's unique point of view on bricks-and-mortar retail may be quite new to you. If his views are half right then this clear guide to the grocery wars is a must-read.

The author is not affiliated with the firms he writes about in this book. But he was a management consultant for many years, taught MBA courses, founded and ran both a national training firm and a software firm, and spent several years in sales. He has an MBA from UCT, a BSc (Hons), a BA, and an ACII.

Plain Press, May 2017

CHAPTER 1: SUMMARY

Topic 1: About the wars

THE END DATE on the title of this book is 2020. Yet I wrote a first draft in 2014, and published this first edition in May 2017. So it's not a history written by an insider. It's more of a forecast made by an outsider.

There is a war going on in the supermarket sector. It's not obvious, in that most of the battles are taking place behind the scenes and too slowly for the naked eye to pick up. The official experts have noticed that there are big changes and have said what they think caused them, but I don't think they go nearly far enough: the changes are so marked that it's like a war between two ways of doing business.

I have no inside knowledge, so my thoughts are based on what I've seen as a shopper and my background in business. I can't say for sure what might have been going on behind the scenes. That's why I made up a Case Study to explore the issues. It let me look at how these wars started, and where they could be by the end of the decade.

In this first topic, I describe the market in broad terms, the share of it that is held by the main groups, and how I expect it will have changed by 2020.

The top four supermarket groups in the UK are Tesco, Sainsbury's, Asda, and Morrison's. They are known as the Big Four. They are losing market share and can't seem to do a thing about it. At the same time, two groups who came from Europe – Aldi and Lidl – are gaining market share as fast as they can open new stores. I've called them the Small Two.

The Small Two have been in the UK for close to thirty years. Their sales have grown fast for much of the time. But only when their market share got to 5pc did the press start to take notice.

It is clear that the Small Two are winning. And it's clear that their gains in market share have been at the expense of the Big Four. The signs are that it will go on this in way, at least until 2020. I think I know why. The Big Four won't like it when they find out, if they don't suspect it already.

We can start with the market share of each group for the three months ended August 2014. The total held by the Big Four was 73pc; by the Small Two it was 8pc; and by the rest of the market it was 19pc (see Topic 10).

My guess is that the Small Two should grab at least twelve percentage points of market share from the Big Four over the next six years. That means the Small Two's share should go up from 8pc to at least 20pc. And the Big Four's share should fall from 73pc to at most 61pc. The market share of the rest should stay about where it is now; they don't play much of a role in this book (see Topic 4).

Where will the growth in Small Two sales come from? By then they should have close to twice as many stores as they had at the start date. That would take their market share to some 17pc. The other 3pc – to take them up to 20pc – should come from the growth in the size of some of their new stores. The Small Two will take this market share from the Big Four; in turn, the

Big Four will shrink both in number of stores and sales per store.

These views may seem to be preposterous. Our supermarkets are some of the best in the world. How can a couple of minnows walk in and take away market share from the big guys – each with more than £10 billion in sales per year – just like that? The experts have not explained why the Big Four seem to be unable to stop the Small Two.

The answers to this are startling. I sum them up in the next topic.

Here's what I think will happen. The wars will lower the cost structure of the whole sector. This includes suppliers as well as the supermarket groups. The main effect will be the gains to shoppers. We don't need to wait until 2020 for the official experts to tell us why; we can see with our own eyes, and can keep tabs on what we spend.

Where will our savings come from?

For some time, the Small Two have been able to sell goods of the same quality cheaper. Their sales are now large enough for the Big Four to feel the pain and look for ways to cut their own long-term costs. That means the Big Four will need to change the way they do business. They must know by now that they risk going broke if they don't. This is partly why prices should freeze or fall. All shoppers should win even if we don't change our habits.

On top of that, inflation may stay quite low in the UK for years. The net result will be that the whole economy – and not just the shopper – should gain billions of pounds a year.

In the rest of this book I describe why this is a war – between two ways of doing business – and not just the same old contest. I describe how it started, why the Small Two are winning, why the Big Four can't do a thing to stop it – even when they know how it works – and what may unfold in the next few years to 2020. To do this, I show how 'keep it small and speed it up' works and why at first it's hard to grasp. I spell out why shoppers stand to gain, and how suppliers and supermarket staff might prepare for the changes.

Some people like to watch the action at sports events. Yet there is more rivalry in commerce than in any sport. We'll see plenty of that in the next few years. In this book I describe some new rules of the grocery game, where we all have ringside seats.

G. N. C. Parker
Diss
May 2017

Topic 2: About this book

MIDWAY THROUGH WRITING my first book – aimed at business owners – I began to write a case study on the supermarket sector in the UK. Soon it dawned on me that it merits a book on its own. More than mere drama, it's like a war zone. But it all takes place in slow motion so you can't see it at first.

That's why I switched to writing what you are reading now. The full story will take six years to unfold; so, much of what you read is guesswork. But at least it may alert those who want to watch it in real time.

Most of these ideas are new in the supermarket sector. I show new ways to look at old facts. I can't say that any one thing in this book is original; it may seem to be new to most readers because of how I've applied it.

The reader does not need to know any maths. Primary school arithmetic is enough to grasp the main themes. It's better to use arithmetic than maths to follow how things work. Once we've done it once it's easy to do it the next time.

I expect most readers to be shoppers, not experts. I use more plain words than jargon so there's no need for readers to have business know-how.

There's a wide range of topics: experts in a topic may want to skim-read it to get the gist, and those for whom it is new may want to read it more slowly.

I don't stand to gain no matter how my guesses turn out. I wrote as a shopper with experience in commerce. I've not looked at the financial statements of any of the firms, nor spoken about it to their staff. I gleaned the facts I needed from the media and from what I've seen in the stores.

I use the Case Study to explore a range of themes and views about issues in this sector. There are two groups in the Case Study. One is a group of firms called Mastt: they are the market leaders. The other is a single firm called Illiad: they are the upstarts. The body of the Case Study comprises a string of meetings, in which two main characters from Illiad trade ideas. The market share data used in the Case Study is the same as that used in the real world.

I don't have much to say about any single firm in the Big Four or Small Two.

The facts on which I base my forecasts are easy to find and check. I quote my sources at the end of each topic, but they can't be blamed for what I say. The results can be checked, starting now.

Topic outline

The book consists of sixty topics in nine chapters. Each topic stands more or less on its own. You may find it best to read it in sequence. Some topics overlap, where I say the same thing but change the angle: the main reason for this is that the key theme in the book is new and worth saying more than once. Fast shopping and small footprint shops have changed the face of grocery retailing because they bring prices down. Those groups that want to survive will need to change too.

The first five chapters are building blocks for the rest of the book. In Chapter 6 we start to look at the 'secrets' and how they work.

Now and then I give some spoilers. That is, I reveal some secrets too early. But it's fine to read them there and then. Like peeling an onion, there's more to follow.

In Chapter 1 (Summary) I spell out the forecast and give a brief spoiler of the secrets that reveal how these wars will be won. I show how Little's Law can be used to work out the gains from fast shopping, how flow rate can boost sales and profit, and the part played by store size.

Chapter 2 (Background) is about what the official experts have left out. That is, why the market changed and why it differs so much from what we've seen before. I run through why we can assume that all the rival groups have been acting on purpose, and where some of them may have erred. I describe the Case Study and sources of the data used in the book. Then I sketch out what this sector looked like in the 90s, and the role played by IT. This touches on why the top firms in this sector in the UK have been admired all over the world.

In Chapter 3 (Shoppers) I look at some key issues. Which should come first, the product or the shopper? Who should the stores aim for, the whole person or their mood when they shop? How big a range of products should stores stock? Can they sell both online and in-store and still hold their margins? What pincer movement can trap the Big Four?

Chapter 4 (Margins) is about what stores don't want to reveal – gross margins. I show how to work out details without the need for high school maths. This part is pivotal to the rest of the book. It shows the speed at which poor choices can lead to ruin. And it shows how tough it is to be in a mature market with tight margins and falling sales. By now the reader should know how to work out the gains from fast shopping. We take this up again in Part 6.

Chapter 5 (Frameworks) shows how we can use frameworks and rules of thumb to gain insight about what's going on in a market, even when we don't know much about it. We first look at the scope of each firm in a sector and how it might differ from the rest. Then we work out their broad strategies. From there we move on to how a firm new to that market can disrupt it. I applied each step to the UK grocery sector. It shows how the Big Four got themselves into a corner in the last few years, and why they will find it hard to get out.

Chapter 6 (Secrets) is where I spill the beans about two of the new key routes to high profits in grocery stores – fast shopping and small size. I show how these can be tied in with a smart use of store brands, and how any retail store can use these ideas to compete with the big guys – as long as they are willing to take the long view. Then I describe how flow rate concepts can be used in practice. I go through how they can help to relieve each of the main bottlenecks. That is, in the shopping process, at the checkout and in the parking area. I point to the best model we know where they swap time for space – the internet.

In Chapter 7 (Issues) I describe other ways in which the top firms may be at risk. Should growth be organic or fuelled by debt? Should goods be sold at a low price or based on deals? Should companies be private or public? Should they use stealth tactics or play open cards? These have all been used to support 'small and fast' ways to beat the leaders.

Chapter 8 (Growth) shows how gearing works and some snags in using it to speed up growth. It shows how a retail firm can use the sale and leaseback of property to make quick profits. It then shows how this can store up risk that they may later regret. I go through why a services firm should watch their profit and loss account more than their balance sheet.

In Chapter 9 (Options) I recap how the war came about, why the Big Four have been so baffled, and what they might do about it. I wrap up with a list, in priority order, of why the Small Two are winning.

Topic 3: Who this book is for

I WROTE THIS book for shoppers, staff in grocery stores, people in commerce and students to enjoy.

At one main shopper per household, there are more than 27m serious shoppers in the UK (see Topic 10). They may have more of a feel for shopping than those who are known as experts. If you are a shopper you might prefer to find out from this book what's going on now than have to wait for the wisdom of hindsight from others. This book may also nudge you to save a bit more cash when you shop.

More than a million people work for supermarkets or for their suppliers. Change in this sector has a direct effect on their jobs. They know what goes on in stores. But they might not know as much as they'd like about the big picture. If you are one of them you may find that you can use some of these ideas in your job.

There is an army of firms that supplies this sector, or is on its fringes. In the next few years, some supermarkets may shrink their range, some may create more store brands, and new groups may pop up. Any change brings new prospects in its wake; the trick is to know it when you see it. If you own a firm, some of the ideas in this book may prompt you to find new niches, or to gear up in advance. And if you run any kind of retail firm you may want to use some of the ideas about flow rate right now.

Indie consultants may spot some fertile niches; there are many sectors and firms where one can use flow rate concepts to add value for clients. It's easy to grasp and can have a dramatic impact on a firm. It's not yet a fad or cult so you have a free hand to use it where it fits. There are ways to learn about it fast [1].

If you're a student or high school pupil, note that there is not much theory in this book. Much of it is opinion. It is not formal enough to be a hypothesis. It may be safer not to believe a word of it. Not until you have checked the facts, sources and logic. I'd like to repeat what Marx said, "who you gonna believe, me or your own eyes [2]?"

In the world of commerce deeds come first and the words that seem to make sense of it come later. Textbooks make it seem that things are cut and dried. One needs to read them to know what went on in the past and in order to invent the future. It's best to know which notions are based on facts. But still, as The Royal Society (founded in 1660) put it: "take nobody's word for it" [3]. More recent advice comes from Mr. Jaggers: "Take nothing on its looks; take everything on evidence. There's no better rule" [4]. This book differs from many others in that you can check most of its ideas at a store near you. To observe is not enough; one needs to test. It may be useful to design and test some of these ideas as a class project.

High school pupils may want to know how commerce creates wealth for all. Part of what you need is a dab of knowledge about how retail works. You can get that here. Part of it you can get each time you go to a grocery store. These stores are like a microcosm of all shops. There's not much to hide: products and prices are in the open for all to see. It's not hard to grasp the magic of trading. It's where all who take part walk away better off than when they started.

Spoiler for students

Take, for instance, a firm on the internet with low running costs. It has hundreds of customers. Say that at the end of six months the firm has ten times as many customers. Yet running costs are still the same. How can this be?

That might not be so hard to work out when it comes to online commerce. But now let's ask this question in the bricks and mortar world. "How can sales go up tenfold with no change in running costs?"

Let's say you own a club and your only running costs are rent for the hall. There is enough space for fifty people and they each pay you a fee to get into your club. Once the fees have covered the rent you start to make a profit. The more people you can fit in the club the more profit you make. The number of people you can fit in the club is called its capacity.

But no-one says you have to fit them all in at the same time. You can fill up the room and empty it a few times in a night. The number of people who go through the room is called the throughput, or flow rate. Let's say the capacity of the club is fifty people. If you fill it up and empty it ten times in a night, the throughput is five hundred people nightly. You'll make much more profit from five hundred people than from fifty.

Or think of water from a river that flows into a dam and then out the other side. Capacity is how much water the dam can hold at one time. Throughput (or flow rate) is how much water flows out of the dam in a period of time.

To measure throughput in a club or grocery store, at the end of each day you count how many people paid at the tills. In broad terms, to make more sales at peak times, we can either make more space to fit in more people, or we can fit in the same number of people more often. We can swap more time for less space.

TOPIC 3 NOTES

[1] See coursera.org/learn/wharton-operations, and Gerard Cachon and Christian Terwiesch, 'Matching Supply with Demand: An Introduction to Operations Management' (New York: McGraw-Hill Irwin, 2006).
[2] Chico Marx: see the 16th (or so) quote on imdb.com/title/ tt0023969/quotes.
[3] See en.wikipedia.org/wiki/Nullius_in_verba.
[4] Charles Dickens, 'Great Expectations' (London: Penguin, 2012/ 1861).

Topic 4: Predictions for 2020

THERE ARE TWO key predictions in this book. The first is that the combined market share of the Small Two in 2020 will be more than twice what it is now. The second is that it will all come at the expense of the Big Four. The market share of the rest of the firms will stay more or less the same.

The date from when we start is August 2014; the date at which we end is August 2020. The date of this first edition of the book is May 2017.

To be more precise, my guess is that from the start date to the end date the market share of the Small Two will grow from 8.4pc to at least 20pc. And that of the Big Four will shrink by a like amount, from 73pc to no more than 61pc (see Topic 10).

To work it out, I started with the 'why's'.

None of the Big Four can compete with the Small Two on price. The running costs of the Big Four are too high and their gross margins are too low.

Running costs include wages and asset costs, such as rent. These costs are high in the Big Four because their stores are big. It's also why their shoppers may take a long time to shop.

This brings us to one of the two big secrets of the Small Two's success. It is that of shopping speed. The faster that shoppers shop, the more sales the store can make at peak times. This means that for the same level of sales as the Big Four, the Small Two's running costs are lower. If we were to use jargon we might say that the secret lies in 'shopper throughput' not in 'size of store.' Or 'flow rate is more important than capacity'.

The other big secret is that the Small Two stock mainly store brands plus a few national brands. The Big Four stock mainly national brands plus some store brands, and they may have to keep doing this for some time. Later, we'll see why.

Store brands drive down the running costs of the Small Two stores. The shopper has the choice of only one or two store brands instead of a full range of rival national brands. Thus the store saves on floor space. But the shopper also takes less time to choose. Thus they shop faster. Both of these factors drive down the running costs for each GBP of sales.

Store brands also yield much higher gross margins than national brands. These can be by up to a third. We'll also see why, later (see Topic 44).

It would be slow and hard work for the Big Four to change their format. Even if they wanted to. This means that the Small Two can go on as they are doing now because they make more operating profit at the same price and quality. It's not likely that the Big Four can match prices, survive a drawn-out price war, or change their way of doing things in less than six years. It means that the market share of the Small Two should keep on growing at the expense of the Big Four.

In the next few years the size of grocery stores will shrink. There will be fewer giant stores like some of those of the Big Four, and more of the small footprint stores like those of the Small Two. Prices will stay down and quality will go up. It will never have been so easy, fast and cheap to shop for basic groceries.

It's quick to write that they should 'keep it small

and speed it up.' It takes a few more lines to show that these two parts are linked – the smaller the size, the less time spent in shopping – but it takes a few pages to describe how it works. That's one of our main themes.

No matter how the changes pan out, shoppers will gain. Yet the effect of these changes on the staff in the sector is not clear. They could have a soft or hard landing. This will depend in each case on what choices the supermarket bosses make.

Making assumptions

So far I've said 'why'; we need some details. I'm going to drill down a touch, to show my assumptions, A1 to A3. The results don't depend on my being precise, so I use round numbers.

The size of the market will stay more or less the same right up to 2020 (A1). How could this occur? One way is for growth in volume to be matched by a fall in prices. The Small Two's low prices may also keep the rest in check. I used £100b as the size of the market at the start date (see Topic 10). Does this matter? Should we care what it turns out to be in 2020? Do I predict that the market size will be £100b? The answer in all three cases is no. I use round figures as a device to help work things out. But I predict market share, not market size. If the Small Two reach 20pc we should not care if market size is one or two hundred billion GBPs. For it to be valid, we just need to measure it in the same way at the end as at the start.

If the market size is £100b, a 20pc share is £20b. It helps that one billion pounds is one per cent. It's easy to work with an amount. So from now on I'll show amounts, not percentages, as they mean the same thing here.

Now we can spell out what I predicted. Can the sales of the Small Two grow from £8.4b to £20b in six years? We can hone it down some more and ask: by how much do the Small Two need to grow each year to reach £20b sales by 2020? (Note that 'k' means a 'thousand' and 'b' a billion. All of the numbers below are 'about'.)

Their sales in real terms would need to grow by between 15pc and 16pc each year [1]. How likely is that? I'll look at them one at a time, starting with Aldi.

In 2014 Aldi said they would open 60 stores in the next year [2]. They had 500 stores at the time; that means 12pc growth in their store count. How close would this sort of growth bring them to our target? Let's drill down a bit more.

Growth in store count is not the same as sales growth. Let's say, to start with, that a store's sales vary in proportion to its size (A2). There are at least five ways that a firm can get real sales growth. The first three are: shoppers spend more on each visit, they shop more often, and more of them shop. Let's say that there is no change in any of these (A3). The other two ways that a firm can get real growth is if they open more stores, and bigger stores. We'll look at these two ways.

Both of these two ways imply that growth in Aldi's sales depends on the floor space that they add in the next six years. Their market share at the start date was 4.8pc. So their sales must have been £4.8b [3]. Say that they added 12pc new stores in each of the next six years. They'd land up with twice what they have now, close to 1000 stores [4]. If their stores stayed the same size, sales would be £9.6b, twice what they are now.

If Lidl grew at the same rate of 12pc each year then their sales would double, to £7.2b. Combined sales of the two would be £16.8b; that's £3.2b shy of our £20b target.

But Aldi has said that their new stores will be bigger than they are now. They will be 1250 sq. metres [5]. Their old stores are 750 square metres.

This means their sales should be more than £9.6b in six years. How much more? The total size of all their stores should be 1000k sq. m. (Old stores 375k sq. m.; plus new stores 625k sq. m. [6]). To get their new sales we should divide the new total size by the old size and then times by 4.8. That is £12.8b [7]: this would give us the £3.2b we're looking for. Combined sales would be £20b in 2020 [8]. Bingo. That makes it easy: both groups grow their store count at 12pc per year, and Aldi's new stores are bigger than their old ones.

Now we must see if this sort of growth is doable.

In the last twenty years [9], Aldi grew from 70 stores (1995) to 550 (2015); that's nearly 11pc growth each year. Lidl grew from 40 stores (1994) to 608 (2014); that's nearly 15pc growth each year.

But these results are skew because the early growth was high. Growth slowed down in recent years [10]. Aldi grew from 289 stores (2005) to 550 (2015); that's growth of some 7pc per year for ten years. Lidl grew from 520 stores (2009) to 608 (2014); that's growth of some 3pc per year for five years.

Part of the glitch in the last few years can be put down to the banking crash of 2008. Since then, the

Small Two's growth rate has speeded up. Like-for-like sales at Aldi grew by 30pc in 2013 [11]. Sales in 2014 grew by 31pc, from £5.3b to £6.9b [12]. Aldi plans to open 93 new stores in 2016, to take them to more than 700 stores – close to 15pc up; Lidl plans to open 78 new stores, close to 13pc up [13]. So they both plan to grow faster than before. It's clear from this that they can meet the forecast.

Dropping assumptions

But if planned growth fails to close the gap, what else can we bring in? We could simply drop some of our assumptions, A1 to A3. For instance, the Small Two could close the gap if they make more sales per square metre per store. Thus, more shoppers visit each store, or they do so more often or they spend more when they get there. Why might this happen?

The Small Two now advertise more than they did in the past. And the press gives free publicity each time they talk about the 'threat from the German discounters'. The changes that the Small Two are making will gain momentum. We can see that they are upping their old targets. As they open more stores and their total footprint grows they should continue to grow. More shoppers will get to sample their wares.

So, just like with all forecasts, we may be wrong; but just like with some forecasts, we should be close.

One more thing: how can I be so sure that the Small Two will grow fast while the rest of the market shrinks or stays static? That's the main thrust of the next few topics.

TOPIC 4 NOTES

[1] Sales of 20b are 2.38 times sales of 8.4b. This is the same as saying that sales of 238 are 2.38 times sales of 100. In six years, 100 grows to 231 at 15% compound; and to 244 at 16% compound. So 100 grows to 238 at between 15% and 16% compound.

[2] A press report said that they planned to open 60 stores in 2014; as it turned out they opened 54: international supermarket news. com/ news/ 19887

[3] Based on 1pc equals £1b. In fact, their sales were reported to be £5.3b in 2013.

[4] At a rate of 12% each year an amount doubles in some six years. To test this, in a plain calculator enter '1.12', 'times', 'times', '100'. Now press 'equals' six times. You should get 197, close to twice as much as 100.

[5] See telegraph.co. uk/ finance/ news by sector/ retail and consumer/ 11127065/ Aldi-interview-the-men-who-have-revolutionised-our-shopping

[6] 500 at 750 sq. m is 375k sq. m; 500 at 1250 sq. m is 625k sq. m.

[7] 1000 divided by 375 times 4.8 is 12.8.

[8] 12.8 plus 7.2.

[9] fooddeserts. org/ images/ suptime NonTesco

[10] See Note [9] above.

[11] See Note [5] above.

[12] See Note [2] above.

[13] See telegraph.co. uk/ finance/ news by sector/ retail and consumer/ 11995280/ Aldi-and-Lidl-plot-to-open-five-times-as-many-new-stores-as-Big-Four.

Topic 5: Summary of secrets

ARE THERE SECRETS that allow the Small Two to charge less than the Big Four for similar products? Here are some quick questions and answers.

Can the Small Two charge less than the Big Four for the same product and yet make more profit? If so, can they do it with no drop in quality? 'Yes' to both questions.

Can they do it by following the mantra 'pile 'em high and sell 'em cheap'? And can they do it by squeezing their suppliers? 'No' to both questions.

Can they do it by cutting running costs? If they can do this and their rivals can't do this, yes. But that's the wrong question. The right question is: how? The answer is one of the secrets.

Can they do it by selling a smaller range of basic goods? That helps.

Can they do it by selling mainly store brands? That helps a lot.

Well then, what's the main secret? The answer lies in a new mantra 'keep it small and speed it up.'

To put it in a few words, if they make the store small, then shopping can be quick. When shopping is quick, at peak times a small store can make the same sales per hour as a bigger store. A small store costs less to run at all times, not just at peak times. One way the Small Two keep their stores small is by selling just a few national brands. They sell mainly store brands. These cost them up to a third less, which cuts down their cost of sales. With more sales and lower costs they can afford to charge low prices that their rivals can't match.

The Small Two are likely to stay ahead for some years. They have nearly a thousand stores in the right places, so the Big Four have a long way to catch up. They might choose not to try and catch up, but to take their loss of market share with good grace.

The mantra might sound so simple that it can't be true. The rest of the book is to show why it is true.

Topic 6: Word usage & notes

WHERE A STORE group gets a supplier to make a brand just for them, I use the phrase 'store brand'; some say 'private label' or 'own brand' or 'house brand'.

The words 'firm', 'business' and 'company' each have their own meaning, and now and then they mean the same thing. Where they do, I stick to 'firm'.

I use feet and yards and, some of the time, metres; 'k' to stand for 'thousand', 'm' for 'million' and 'b' for billion; 'data' and 'sales' as singular or plural.

Whether a store group owns or rents their stores, I speak of 'rent'. It's a cost they have to bear in one way or another: real or calculated.

Here are my abbreviations:

- aka: also known as
- b: billion
- Bogof: buy one get one free; see also HLP
- bookies: bookmakers
- CEO: boss of a firm
- EDLP: everyday low pricing
- FMCG: fast moving consumer goods
- GBP: Great Britain pound (money)
- GDP: Gross domestic product (money)
- HLP: high-low pricing; see also bogof
- indie: independent
- IP: intellectual property
- IT: information technology
- k: thousand
- m: million

- mean: average
- Ops Mgmt.: Operations management
- owner-run firm: may be a private company*
- pc: per cent
- PC: personal computer
- plc: public (limited) company
- SKU: stock-keeping unit
- spec: specification

*in which case it is 'limited'

I don't expect readers to know about accounting but it's fine if they do. So I don't use formal terms unless I have to. I explain what I mean by the words as I go along. My hope is that readers get what I mean with ease. Accountants should know what I mean from the context.

Some of the words I use in this book are in the list below. I use the words on the left, not those in brackets on the right. Here's the list:

- Sales (aka turnover, revenue)
- Cost of sales (aka cost of goods sold)
- Gross profit: 'GP' (sales minus cost of sales)
- Running costs (aka operating expenses)
- Operating profit ('GP' minus running costs)

There are a few more items on the list, but I hardly use them in this book. Here they are:

- Non-operating costs (non-operating expenses)
- Profit before interest and tax (PBIT; EBIT)
- Interest and tax
- Net profit (i.e. PBIT minus interest and tax)*

* (aka net income)

Later on I describe some more terms used in the profit and loss account and the balance sheet (see Topic 21). But here I explain the use of the word 'stock' – and not the word 'inventory' – to mean 'goods for resale.'

In the UK if you want to buy a share of a public company (plc) you buy shares in that company. The way they describe it in UK balance sheets is that the company issues 'Ordinary shares' [1]. But in the USA, if you want to buy a share of a public company you buy stock in that company. The way they describe it in USA balance sheets is that the company issues 'Common stock' [2].

Thus in the UK you buy shares and in the USA you buy stock. In the USA they use the word 'inventory' (and not 'stock') to mean goods for resale; by so doing there is less chance for them to get confused about what is meant by the word 'stock.' (Some people in the UK also use the word 'stock' to mean 'shares' in a UK company.)

The accounting bodies in the UK, the USA and other countries like to use the same words. It gives them a common standard so that they know what the other one means. But some words are so entrenched it is hard to see how they will manage to agree on which to use. For instance, it may prove hard to decide which to use as the standard: 'ordinary shares' or 'common stock'. The UK and the USA would each want to stay with what they've got. So in the UK they may stay with 'shares' for a long time to come; and in the USA they may stay with 'stock.'

Most big UK firms now use 'inventory' in place of 'stock' to mean 'goods for resale'. But many nonaccounting people in the UK still use 'stock' to mean 'goods for resale.' For them it's always been that way. So that's why I use 'stock' in this edition.

Sources

In the text I refer to my sources for each topic with a number in square brackets. For instance: [1] or [2] and so on. The Note on sources is at the end of each topic, not at the end of the book. This is to make it easy to find in the ebook as well as in the printed book. Some readers may want to check a source, to settle their own minds; or they may want to explore that topic in more detail at a later stage. But for the rest of the readers, don't bother. There's not much detail in the Notes. It's mostly in the text.

One source is Wikipedia. An article may have changed since I last called it up. So the reader might not read the same words that I did. This is one of those things; it is how it works. Yet Wikipedia is a good place to start. And their list of references at the end of each entry is handy.

In my Notes I have cut off the first part of all URLs (like http and www); this is so that links won't be live if this book is read in a browser. But if the reader wants to follow the link, they should copy and paste the truncated URL into their search engine. The correct URL should show up in the search engine results.

Index

There are no page numbers in the ebook. The index of both the ebook and the printed book refers to topic numbers and not to page numbers. Topics are numbered from 1 to 60.

TOPIC 6 NOTES

[1] See 'FRS 102 Illustrative Financial Statements': ey. com/ Publication/ vwLUAssets/ EY-FRS-102-illustrative-financial-statements/ %24FILE/ EY-FRS-102- illustrative-financial-statements. pdf

[2] Robert N Anthony, David F Hawkins, Kenneth A Merchant, 'Accounting: Text and Cases' (New York: McGraw-Hill Irwin, 2007).

CHAPTER 2: BACKGROUND

Topic 7: No bobbing corks

THERE HAS BEEN a slow change in the way people shop for groceries in the last few years. It's been like a wave that starts as a swell and then grows. The wave began to break in 2014. It should have run its course by 2020.

The Big Four have been losing sales to the Small Two and it looks like that will continue. Why? The official experts seem to think that the answer is because shopping habits have changed.

Shoppers spend more than £100b on groceries each year (see Topic 10). This is big enough to grip the minds of the experts. They might have seen the change in shopping habits – but not its causes. Why not? Perhaps the first reasons they thought of seemed to explain it. So why look for more?

But once we start to look in detail we find a horde of real causes. The experts don't seem to have seen these. They have seen 'what' but not 'why'.

Here are some of the things the experts seem to agree on. In the last two decades the Big Four opened a lot of big new stores, many of them out of town. They would have known that in the long term they couldn't grow faster than the market as a whole. And that once the sector had too much floor space then the whole market would suffer. They might have thought they still had more time; or else that snags would strike their rivals first. When the banking crash hit in 2008, perhaps they should have paused in their drive for more and bigger stores.

Experts suggested some causes of the malaise and/or what to do about it. Outside forces changed the market at a faster rate than the Big Four changed. More people now shop on the internet. The 'cuts' caused people to spend less; now they count the pennies and shop at the 'German discount stores'. Habits have changed in that fewer people do a big shop each week [1].

Does that mean that these vast grocery firms are like bobbing corks? That they were caught in a perfect storm? Did no-one act on purpose? All this time, was it just events that drove the market?

I don't think these events were the real causes of the malaise in the sector. They just made the real causes worse. Real causes are those that explain not what happened but why it happened. These don't all come from outside. They can come from choices made by the Big Four and the Small Two in the last two decades. Surely if the Big Four were victims of outside events they would have worked out how to deal with them by now? Press reports claimed that some of the Big Four don't know how to fix their problems. This would mean they don't know what the real causes are. But to fix them they have to know what the real causes are.

It doesn't help to blame the bosses. What if the Small Two had a unique way to cut costs? One that let them sell the same products for less than their rivals? The rival stores would not be able to match these prices no matter what their bosses did. So it would be of no use to fire the bosses.

Official experts explained how the Big Four lost

ground, but not why the Small Two gained this same ground. Nor why the Big Four aren't able to do the same things as the Small Two. Nor why they can't stop the Small Two from taking their market share.

It took some time to sink in that the ideal strategy had changed. Now it is the reverse of what it was in 1995. Big isn't better, it's worse. The grocery store should be close to, not out of, town. Experts explained how the structure of the market has changed. Then they said that this was the cause of the problems. But mere changes in the structure of a market can't be a cause of its problems.

The real snags arose when firms failed to respond to changes in the structure of the market. To solve them the firms need to change their own structures. To do that, they have to change their strategies [2].

There are signs (October 2016) that some of them have started to change their fixed cost structure. This seems to be on the right track. It's a more thoughtful response than just to cut prices. Their shareholders might insist that these firms can't just act like bobbing corks and hope for the best. They are going to have to do much more to change their strategies. But it's going to take them until at least 2020 to make the new strategies work.

All this time it's been at the top of shoppers' lists that, when they buy basics, they want (next to low prices) to get it done fast [3]. This has been ignored by most of the official experts. It means that we have to delve deeper to come up with the real causes of the malaise.

TOPIC 7 NOTES

[1] There are numerous articles about this on the internet. One can use search terms such as supermarkets, discounting, grocery sector and retail.
[2] See en.wikipedia. org/ wiki/ Structure follows strategy and en.wikipedia. org/ wiki/ Form follows function
[3] See David Walters & Jack Hanrahan, 'Retail Strategy' (UK: MacMillan Business, 2000), 253.

Topic 8: Acting on purpose

I ASKED MYSELF, what if these firms have been acting on purpose all this time? What if they each had their own way of doing things? What if the way that the Small Two do things allows them to keep their prices way below those of their rivals? For the same quality. With no need to squeeze their suppliers. And in such a way that their rivals are not going to be able to change in less than six years, even if they wanted to?

The more I watched how each store group worked the more it seemed that I was on the right track. So I assumed that they had been acting on purpose. Then I thought, what would the Small Two have had to do to meet the aims set out above? I tried to look for the most likely reasons and not just accept the first plausible ones.

Let's say that a couple of decades ago one of the Big Four firms crafted a smart strategy. It was so good that all their rivals copied them. It worked well for the next twelve years, until soon after the banking crash in 2008. Then it stopped working, but the Big Four didn't notice. That's fair enough. If it doesn't seem to be broke, keep going.

Let's say that in the same period the Small Two chose strategies that were a success and stayed that way. They got it right. Then they stayed in tune with the changes in shoppers' needs. They added new stores and are now big enough for the Big Four to notice.

It may simply be that the Big Four used a good approach for too long. Whereas the Small Two used a good approach that started well and still works well. The snag for the Big Four is that now they are too bound up in what they are doing to be able to change fast. So they will find it hard to compete with the Small Two even if they wanted to.

The words 'cause' and 'purpose' don't mean the same thing. An outside force that changes something can be said to be a cause of the change. The cause may or may not be a person. It can be an event or set of events. But only a person can act on purpose. First, they want to change something; second, they act to bring it about. It might not change in the way that they wanted but they still acted on purpose.

Both a bobbing cork and a ship can float on the sea. Which way the bobbing cork goes depends on out-side causes, such as the current and the winds. Which way the ship goes depends on the purpose in the minds of the captain and crew.

Working backwards

This all led me to assume that the Big Four and Small Two had acted with a sense of purpose. I wasn't privy to how any of them thought, so I had to work backwards. I started with where they are now, and worked back to see what sort of logic might have got them here.

For both sides, I imagined what they might have thought and done in the past to get where they are now.

This approach is often used in commerce and in war. And it's been used as a thinking aid in other walks of life [1]. We work out what might have taken place in the past based on what we can see now. We assume they were acting on purpose even if they weren't.

The entrance to a Small Two store is a good place to start. Why is there only one entrance for a trolley? Why are the aisles so narrow? How wide are they, and why? Why do all the stores have the same layout? Why don't they try to draw shoppers to the back of the store with special offers? Why are there no bogofs? Why should shoppers pack their goods once they have paid, away from the checkout?

We could pose scores of questions. Dumb ones are best. All we need is some curiosity and know-how. We have these by virtue of being shoppers. We should note how a Small Two store does something; then how a rival Big Four store does that same thing. If the Small Two store does it in a different way, assume that they did it their way on purpose. Then try to work out why. It's a simple cheat sheet but it works.

We should first list as many questions as we can think of. Walking through a store can act as a prompt. We can leave answers until later. We can't expect to come up with right answers until we've looked at the data/facts. We should ask a broad range of questions to know which facts to look for in the first place.

When we start to answer each question we should keep asking 'why' [2]. We keep working backwards until asking 'why' doesn't work. That means there's a good chance the previous answer is a first cause. Until then we are dealing with symptoms. After doing it a few times one gets the knack. A few times more and it becomes a skill. It seems that to do it well one doesn't need a big brain, just practice.

There's no need to choose between views that clash with each other. We can find good research to back up any view. We should keep all ideas on the go as long as they are useful, or until we are sure they aren't.

We may get the same answer to a range of questions. Thus we may get the answer 'to save rent' to more than one question. The question may relate to aisle width, product range, standard size, store size, aisle displays, and so on. Then we should look at the issue of rent in more detail. Is it a major cost item for them? How much? What is it as a percentage of sales?

Some answers may be linked with others. For instance, there may be some answers that sound the same as 'to save rent', such as, 'to save wages'. Both may be part of a broader heading such as, in this case, 'to save fixed costs'.

This is in fact exactly what I found. A lot of questions could be answered by 'to save on fixed costs'. Yet this didn't quite chime with the clear attempt by the Small Two to make sure that their checkout was fast. I thought that fast checkout must be related to shopping speed. But this fits in more with an aim to speed up sales than to reduce costs. Then it dawned on me that the same thing that caused more sales was also a cause of lower unit cost. And that same thing was fast shopping. So which came first? The desire for faster sales or for less cost?

Then I clicked that it all had to do with flow rate.

Chicken and egg

If a store gets more sales 'per square metre per day' it will result in more sales for the store as a whole. Or, try the other way round. It will result in lower fixed costs per square metre per day for each pound (GBP) of sales.

The two ways to look at the data – more sales or lower unit cost – are connected. So it's chicken and egg.

You may have more sales in the same time period; or the same sales in a shorter period. Either way it means lower fixed costs per GBP of sales.

We bring time into the frame when we link the idea of 'how much' in one period of time. We can see it as linked to speed. High volume in a fixed time period is part of the larger idea of 'flow'. We 'speed up the rate at which we earn sales' to spread our fixed costs so that our profit goes up for each GBP of sales.

I wondered if they had meant this all along. Or should we care? Wasn't it enough that this way of doing things came about from sixty years of relentless effort?

The last step was to apply concepts about 'flow' to the Small Two way of doing things. The concept of 'flow rate' comes from other fields of study. They know a lot about how it works [3]. Thus we don't need to invent what to do from scratch.

For instance, it helps to know that if the snag seems to be one of flow rate then there is one best place to start. That is, find the bottlenecks and try to remove them, one at a time [4]. However, now we have to work backwards. We can see the solutions – those things being done at the Small Two stores – with our own eyes. We need to work out what were the bottlenecks that gave rise to these solutions.

We can see that lots of things that are done by the Small Two take place at the checkouts. Most of them help to remove congestion. The next step is to measure and test. The Small Two might not let us experiment in their stores, but we can observe. (It's clear that checkouts can be the cause of bottlenecks in any kind of shop.)

The steps I suggest might not be the best ones. But they may be of use in thinking about the issues. This applies to any models used in this book. Models can't solve a problem, but they can help define it.

This proviso does not apply to my guesses about market share at the end of the decade; I'll stand by those, even if they turn out to be wrong. But if my guesses turn out to be spot on that doesn't mean that my thinking about their causes is correct. And vice versa. That's the snag with the future. One might predict it right for all the wrong reasons.

TOPIC 8 NOTES

[1] See en.wikipedia. org/ wiki/ Intentional_stance and Daniel C. Dennett, 'The Intentional Stance' (Cambridge Massachusetts: MIT Press, 1989).
[2] See also en.wikipedia. org/ wiki/ 5_Whys
[3] See coursera. org/ learn/ wharton-operations/ lecture/ rjw9P/ flow-rate-inventory-and-flow-time
[4] See also coursera. org/ learn/ wharton-operations / lecture/ lPCJy / finding-the-bottleneck.

Topic 9: Illiad Case Study

THE UK SUPERMARKET wars are like a real-life case study. A lot of things are going on behind the scenes but no-one knows what they all are. I made up my own case study to explore some of them. It has four aims.

First, we can make a mental model of what we think is going on. If we don't know all the facts we can start by making some of them up. This helps when we don't know what will take place in the future. But it also helps when we don't know what took place in the past. After all, when we deal with an uncertain future we don't know what it will look like. But while we don't know what took place in the past at least we know what its future looks like, namely the present position.

Second, we can explore themes that as a rule we might not do. To work in stealth mode, is it better to have a private firm or a plc? Might what is good for shareholders clash with what is good for shoppers? Might what is good for managers clash with what is good for shareholders? If the sector fragments, would small chains do well on the high street? How can the big firms (and their staff) have a soft landing? Is there a best way for small suppliers to thrive? Are there gaps in online commerce that can be filled by bricks and mortar stores?

Third, we can explore big issues using small data. At what rate would the Small Two need to grow to have 20pc market share by 2020? In terms their past growth rate is that viable? Or we could compare the rates of growth of Aldi and Lidl. Why might these rates of growth differ?

Fourth, we can use fictional people to weigh up a range of views.

That's what I did. I made a mental model based on market share data and on things I'd seen in the course of shopping. This gave me some idea of what might be going on. I thought about a set of subject areas that I know about. They became the topics in this book. In each topic I played around with two or more sets of ideas. I put in some ideas that had worked in the past with my clients in various sectors, or that I'd heard or read about. Then I searched for some data to check my conclusions. Such as, what are the facts about checkout speed? What are the gross margins for each group? I had to be able to compare Big Four and Small Two data. But I didn't need much data, and the rest I made up. My list of sources shows which is which.

I have no inside knowledge. So I could not write about the real market. But fiction gave me more scope. (Most of those who really do have inside knowledge can't write about it. They would have lost those rights when they first joined their firms.)

At first I did not see how a store group that is small, and where it is fast and cheap to shop, could be a threat to huge firms. Once I had worked through it I saw that it's more than just plausible: it's compelling. But the change is such a clear break with the past that I can see why it would be easy to miss.

Earlier I said that firms that act with some purpose are like ships. Retail firms in the sector are like a fleet of ships, hard to divert from its chosen course. The mast of a ship can be seen from far away. A market leader is rather like the mast of a ship.

In the Illiad Case Study there are two sides at war. One is the group of market leading firms. I've called the leading firms Mastt (with two 't's). To remind me, the first four letters are the same as the first letters of the Big Four.

The other side in this war is Mastt's rival, a single firm. They came from abroad in the late eighties. This firm worked slowly and with no fuss, to gain a place in the market. They charged low prices from the start. I called them Illiad (with two 'l's). To remind me, it contains anagrams of the names of the Small Two.

Illy Illiad is one of the founders of his firm. His consultant in the UK is Homer Glass. The case study consists of extracts of meetings the two of them had from time to time from 1995. In this book, if a topic has a 'year' in its title – such as 1996 – then it's to do with one of their meetings.

When I refer to the Big Four or the Small Two it's about the real world. When I refer to Mastt or Illiad it's about the Case Study, which is all fiction. I use the same broad market data in the Case Study as in the real world. In the next topic we look at some of this data.

Topic 10: Market data

WE NEED ONLY a few hard facts about the groceries sector. We need current and recent sales figures for the Big Four; the same for the Small Two; plus the totals for the sector. This is all we need to work out the market share for each and how they've changed.

The data I use is from Kantar Worldpanel [1]. I have rounded it to two digits. Their data is clear and consistent and is used by most of the press. They collect their own data, so their numbers may not be the same as those from other sources. They give amounts as well as the market share for each of the firms. I'll use their data from now on and to check the final results.

I took the twelve weeks to 17 August 2014 as the start date.

The Big Four firms are Tesco, Asda, Sainsbury's, and Morrison's. The share of the market held by each of them was 29pc, 17pc, 16pc, and 11pc. That adds up to 73pc. The Small Two firms are Aldi and Lidl. The share of the market held by them was 4.8pc and 3.6pc. That adds up to 8.4pc. We can round this to 8pc.

So the total market share of the Big Four and the Small Two was 81pc.

The market share held by the Big Four had fallen slightly in that year. But the share held by the Small Two had grown to make up for it.

I ignored Waitrose in this book. It's more of a niche brand so it should not change much. Their market share had hardly grown at all in that year. I also left out the Co-op: it had not yet found a new role.

Total grocers' sales in the sector for the three months at the start were £24.7b. If we times by four we get close to £100b. We can use this as a rough market size for 2014. This is fine to work with for the time being. If £100b equals 100pc then each £1b equals 1pc.

How big is £100b? It's hard to get one's head around even £1b. If we used £1 notes it would take one of us more than 30 years to count to £1b. We want to know how much £100b is per person in the UK.

To start with, how big is one billion? In the UK it's now the same as in the USA. A thousand times a thousand is a million. And a thousand times a million is a billion. It also works in reverse. So a billion divided by a million is a thousand.

Now we can work out how much £100b is per person. If there were 100m people in the UK it would work out at £1000 each. But there are only 63m people in the UK. So to work out how much it is per person we should divide 1000 by 0.63. If we round the answer we get £1600.

This works out at some £30 per week per person. There are some 2.3 people in each household [2]. That means each household spends some £70 per week [3].

How much will be spent in 2020? Does it matter? Our concern is market share. That is a percentage. If prices go up due to inflation then market share for each firm should stay the same – all boats rise with the tide. So market size does not matter.

We'll do the same to get a quick fix on the market size in 2020. We'll take four times the three months ending in August. At that time, what we'll want to know is the percentage share held by each of the six firms. As worked out by Kantar Worldpanel, not by us. Let them be the judge [4].

For now, we can see that £100b is easy to work with. We don't need to use a spreadsheet, but if we did we could set it up at the start with round numbers. We could see how they work with each other and how they react when we change them. The main thing is that each billion GBP in sales is a one per cent share of the market.

TOPIC 10 NOTES

[1] See kantar world panel. com/ global/ News/ Grocery-price-inflation-virtually-vanishes-in-the-UK and then click on 'Download the press release for additional data', which shows the press release of 27 August 2014 and the table labelled 'Market Share - Total till roll'.
[2] In 2011 there were 26.4 million households in the UK, and the average household size was 2.3 people. See ons.gov. uk/ people population and community/ population and migration/ population estimates/ bulletins/ population and household estimates for the united kingdom/ 2011-03-21# 2011-census-population-and-household-estimates-for-the-united-kingdom-march-2011
[3] To check. Start with 100 thousand; divide it by 63 to get 1587; divide this by 52 to get 30.52; round this to 30. Then, 30.52 times 2.3 is 70.20; round this to 70.
[4] Here is an update, some two years from the start: uk.kantar. com/ consumer/ shoppers/ 2016/ september-kantar-worldpanel-uk-grocery-share.

Topic 11: Ops Mgmt: the 90s

To grasp the scale of the changes taking place now, we should first look at some that took place in the nineties.

Before that time, control of stock was a problem for all firms that carried it. The holding cost could be up to thirty per cent of its cost price, each year. Yet they had to hold a wide range of stock to attract customers.

The problem lasted as long as it was seen as just an accounting issue. Once firms looked at it from a wider point of view, they began to solve it. This wider point of view was the job of Ops Mgmt. Control of stock formed just a part of what they had to do. To cut down the cost of goods they had to cut the costs of moving them from the supplier to the shelves in the store. The less time taken at each step the less the goods would cost them by the time they reached the shelves.

How much did they cut costs? Stock levels can be measured by how many weeks they take to sell. If cost of sales is £10k per week and stock on hand is £50k, then stock on hand is 'five weeks of sales'. There was a huge drop in stock on hand in UK supermarkets from 1980 to 1996. The ratio went from 5.1 to 1.5 weeks of sales. That's a fall of more than 70pc [1].

Most of this change was thanks to IT. The wider point of view was needed to frame the problem, but it was IT that did the donkey work. IT did not just help to shift the cost of carrying stock from the store to the supplier. It cut the length of the pipeline so that there was no cost to carry. From then on, stock control became a small issue for large firms.

To control stock we first need to observe and then to predict. If we knew which items shoppers want to buy, we could have them ready on the shelves. Thus if we know the demand we can set up the supply. IT keeps track of goods in real time so we can observe what's going on, and it adds things up fast so we can predict and plan what we need to do.

In the nineties there was a shift in the way firms could serve their customers. Drucker had said years before that the chief aim of a firm should be to create and keep a customer [2]. This is not just making a sale. It's to make sure that the customer comes back for more. It was no longer good enough just to push products. With the advances in IT, retail firms could now match shopper needs with product features.

To recap, IT helped firms to do things that they had not even dreamed of. Firms could cut the costs to buy, hold and move stock in the supply chain [3]. And they could match their brands with shopper needs, often one-to-one. The top retail firms in the UK transformed the way they did things. In so doing they kept ahead of most countries in the world.

Display by category

There was one more thing that IT let retail firms do for the first time. This was part of a deeper change that has been under way since the sixties. It was to shift the power to choose what to consume from the huge FMCG firms to the shopper. Not far, but some way.

At one time grocers grouped their products on the shelves by supplier. The big FMCG firms urged stores to give them the best shelf space for their brands.

In return, they might have let the stores take months to pay their bills; it was like giving them loans with no interest. Or they might have given the stores big discounts for bulk orders.

With the choice of shelf space, an FMCG firm could place its own brands next to each other on the shelves. It could offer their own special deals to shoppers. For a few minutes the shopper was a captive. It was a way for the big firms to keep control of what shoppers bought. Small suppliers found it hard to get good shelf space.

Shoppers did not like it but it was all there was. They would have liked to first look for the category – say jam – and only then for the brand. It was a bind to have to first check the shelves of all of the suppliers to see what jams each of them had for sale.

Once again IT made it easy to change. In the stores, they could group stock on the shelves by category [4]. Not by supplier. Why would this be such a big deal? It was more in line with how shoppers liked to shop. They could go straight to the jam category and see jams from all suppliers in one spot. They would have all the brands in front of them before they had to make their choice. It suited the retailer, who could arrange the shelves as they liked. They worked out that they could make more profit this way. That's what they set out to do.

So why was the concept so slow to take off?

The huge FMCG firms didn't like it. It took away a lot of their power. Their brands would have to stand on the shelves next to those of their rivals. They would have to compete for shelf space on price and merit.

These FMCG firms were also not keen to share plans for their own brands with the retailers. Why not? The retailers might pass on their data to other suppliers. Or they might play one off against the other to get cut-price deals. Or, worst of all, they might use this knowledge to boost sales of their own store brands.

The small suppliers, too, might have been afraid. Stores could cut down their range of brands, or choose one big supplier to make all their store brands. It might have meant that the small guys would be dropped.

This lack of trust slowed things up. But at some stage what worked best for the shopper had to win. Stores knew that if they were too slow to act their own rivals would get ahead. As long as there are firms in the market that want and are able to compete, the leading firms can't just keep things as they are: they won't get away with it once shoppers catch on. (We should hold that thought).

For a while it seemed that the FMCG firms had lost and the retail stores had won. Power had moved closer to the shopper, but not all the way. The stores still had the power to choose what to stock in the first place. And the shopper had more choice than before.

How did IT help to force such a big change?

When a store sold an item – of a stock keeping unit (SKU) – it was scanned at the till. The amount in stock of each SKU would be updated in real time. The system could track and try to predict sales. SKU sales data would go direct from retail tills to suppliers. They could then fulfil their own orders. Goods could go straight from there to the retail shelves.

IT also helped stores to track actual sales per

square metre of shelf space. This helped them to decide where to place goods. It made more sense than to base it on the size of bulk discounts offered by FMCG firms.

Signs that there had been a big shift began to appear. Some FMCG firms changed their structure. Before, they had grouped it around their own brands. Now they grouped it around product categories. Such a big change in structure is a sure sign of a change in strategy [5]. (We'll see later how the FCMG firms took back some of the high ground).

The battle was for billions of pounds. Few shoppers knew about it but they still scored from it. Just like today. We don't see each little change as it occurs. But over a long period, when we can compare the old and the new, we can see how much we scored.

Who wins from change?

It is hard to compare old and new costs because inflation warps past prices. But we can try. For instance, we can compare the cost of groceries with wages from one year to the next. Today in the UK we spend about a tenth of our wages on groceries [6]. That means that nine tenths is left for us and the taxman. What was this fraction in 1960? Was it also a tenth? This may come as a shock. It was about a quarter [6]. That shows there's been a huge fall in what we spend on groceries. Clearly, the poorest have gained the most. They spend more of each pound that they earn on basic groceries. So the more these costs fall, the more the poorest score [7].

The change in retail today is as big as that in the nineties. But now more people know that it's going on. Even if they are not yet quite sure what it is. Once we know what to look for we can watch the focus of power shift from supplier to shopper. The shopper is freer to choose what to buy: when, how, for how much, where and from whom.

There is some irony in the change we are now seeing. Thanks to cheaper IT, every shop, no matter how small, can track their SKUs. So the big retail stores no longer have the upper hand. Shoppers no longer need to buy all the things they want at one shop. Like before, they can buy a bit here and a bit there. Twenty years ago IT made sure that 'big' had the edge. Now IT has made sure that 'big' no longer has the edge. Small is the new big.

This, then, is a backdrop to where the market is now.

To see who is winning the war, we need to look at market share. We won't see it if we look in the stores. If a store loses 12pc of its market share in six years that's 2pc a year. We won't notice in our own home store that there are two people less per hundred than there were last year. It will look pretty much the same as before. We need market share to tell us what all these small changes add up to.

Discounters have played a role all this time. But we should not be fooled. Some discounters of the past are market leaders today. Up to the end of the eighties discount stores used a mantra to describe the way they worked. It was called 'pile 'em high and sell 'em cheap.' They kept big piles of stock to lower the risk of running out. But, later, IT solved that problem. Stores tracked sales of their SKUs and restocked more often. It was a new way to keep costs low and save space. The concept of the discount store changed. The old mantra might still have been bandied about; it's a catchy soundbite. But the problem that it solved has long since ceased to exist. Today it's a relic of that past.

TOPIC 11 NOTES

[1] But see Carlo Morelli, 'Britain's Most Dynamic Sector? Competitive Advantage in Multiple Food Retailing' (Business and Economic History 26, no. 2, 1997), 776. jstor. org/ stable/ 23703070. He quotes a stock turnover rate 24 times a year for the then market leaders, some two weeks of sales.

[2] Peter F Drucker, 'The Practice of Management' (Oxford: Routledge, 2011/1955).

[3] See also en.wikipedia. org/ wiki/ Supply_chain

[4] Stores that carry mostly store brands, such as the Small Two, are well placed to manage stock by category. See also en.wikipedia. org/ wiki/ Category_ management

[5] Structure follows strategy: see Note [2] in Topic 7.

[6] Ed Garner, Communications Director of Kantar Worldpanel, at a talk to the National Farmers Union: Consumers and the future Vision of Retail, circa 2014.

[7] So why do most of us seem to be no better off? Other living costs have not gone down: such as the costs of energy, transport and housing. Government has not yet learned how to manage these monopolies. It has also not yet fixed the mess from the banking crash of 2008.

Topic 12: Mktg Mgmt: the 90s

RETAIL IS LIKE a coin. Its two sides are what product or service the firm sells, and who they sell it to.

'Operations' deals with what they sell. The focus is inwards, facing the firm, and the key is to be efficient. It was the core of the last topic. 'Marketing' deals with who they sell to: the shopper. The focus is outwards, facing the market, and the key is to be effective. It's the core of this topic.

To show some of what they focused on in the nineties we can go through a checklist that they used then. Then we can see how well this has held up over time. As before, the reader should be the best judge of how well they did. There were four items on the list. They are the product range, the experience, price and convenience [1].

First on the list was the **product range**. Shoppers liked to have a wide choice. The store could keep track of a huge range of stock thanks to the wonders of IT.

Next on the list was **the experience**. Much of this rests on the physical side. Such as the feeling of space, the layout and the way that goods are displayed. It also rests on the mix of services. Such as the range of offers, restaurants and the way that refunds are dealt with.

Third on the list was **pricing**. Apart from its usual role, price acts as a signal to the kind of shopper that the store aims for: its target market. The price is there to tell their target market that the store would suit them. When all products are basic goods, prices of rival brands tend to be quite close to each other. There is not much room for a grocery store to use 'price' as a way to differ from its rivals.

A store group would choose their price tactic. It may be HLP, bogof or EDLP. But it needs to suit their target market. Shoppers who link price with quality may not go for EDLP; they may believe that 'you get what you pay for'. Others may like the chance to snap up bargain bogofs.

With the new IT, stores could combine a vast product range with low prices. They and their shoppers could have the best of both. Stores could have as tight a control on their gross margins as when they had a narrow range. Before the new IT, shoppers had to go to specialist stores to buy luxury goods; now they could buy them all at the one store.

Fourth on the list was **convenience**. Part of this is the location of the store. It should be quick to get to, with easy access and parking.

In the light of this list we can check how well the market leaders were doing by the nineties.

They had made three vital choices to do with the product range. All were enabled by IT. One, they boosted their range from a few thousand to tens of thousands of SKUs. The shopper at that time looked on in awe. It was a feast for the eyes and mind. One could call it the Aladdin's Cave effect. They might leave the store with less than twenty items, yet it was a heady experience for them to have had the choice from a range of forty thousand items sourced from all over the world.

Two, stores carried more store brands. These

gave them higher gross margins than they got from national brands. In part, they kept their national brands
as a yardstick for shoppers to gauge the value of their
store brands.

Three, they upped their range of non-grocery
lines (for instance, clothes). This changed their product
mix. These lines gave them higher gross margins than
they got from their grocery lines.

Both of these last two changes – more store
brands and more non-grocery lines – raised their gross
margins. It gave them more room to give discounts and
keep their image for low prices.

These three changes helped the first three items
on our list. (They are the product, the price and the experience).

To boost the fourth item on our list, that of convenience, they moved some of their stores out of town.
The new lines needed a lot of space. There was ample
space at a low rent out of town. There were no rival
stores to distract shoppers; they could shop at one store
rather than drive miles to shop at others. Stores used
loyalty cards to get to know more about their shoppers'
needs.

These features all helped to bring in the sense of
the one-stop shop. In a short time these had morphed
into shopping destinations. In those days, stores vied to
be the shoppers' 'primary choice'. That is a store at
which a shopper spends more than 50pc of their budg-
et. Shoppers who shopped at out-of-town stores were
captive. They found it convenient to do all their shopping in one place.

At the time these turned out to be good choices

for the market leaders. But there were some snags to one-stop shopping, which grew as years went by. These should give us a clue as to why their model might have failed.

Pros and cons

Not all retail is the same. Basic goods are not the same as luxuries. They aren't bought in the same way. People like to shop for basics fast, and then get out [2]. They want to take their time when they buy luxuries. There may be a clash when they try to do both at once. One-stop shopping can create a mental tug of war.

If shoppers tire of the one-stop shop, might they prefer to buy from a range of local shops? If they could buy at the same price or better? If so, what would happen to the giant stores on the edge of town?

Then there's the impulse buy. That's not the same as buying luxuries or basics. The mood of the shopper depends on what they are shopping for. They might have a range of shopping 'missions'. Their mood would match their mission in each case. So, it can be a snag if a store tries to be all things to all shoppers – at the same time.

It would be awkward to have to have a range of store types, to suit a range of shopper types. If a store group has both giant and convenience stores they may need to keep track of a range of target markets and moods. The strategies for each would not be the same. These may overlap and change over time. As it gets more complex, it may confuse the shopper.

One more snag is, what happens once all store groups do the same thing? The Aladdin's Cave effect may be the first to go. Does the shopper really want to choose from a range of 40k goods when they buy only twenty? Do they need the miles of aisles? The long trek to and from their car?

A key to a good strategy is that it hangs together. Each part should both stand firm on its own and also work in concert with the rest. The UK supermarkets did all of that. At first sight, the way each part of the strategy links to the next one is a plus. A big range of products leads to more space and a yet bigger range. It leads to out of town stores with no near rivals.

This sort of 'tight coupling' works well until one part goes wrong [3]. It may not be easy to fix just the one part. They may be forced to undo all the others. What if shoppers no longer want to do one big shop each week? If they want a quick in-out for their groceries, and a slow stroll when they shop for luxuries?

Store groups may find that a modular structure beats one with tight coupling. It lets them change one part on its own and leave the rest intact. It helps them to change course quickly. And it matters less if they get it wrong the first time.

It would seem that this last snag stands out from all the rest. The Big Four should have had a Plan B to exit from all or part of their strategy at short notice should the need arise. And to do so in such a way that they don't disturb any other part of it. It may be the fact that they could not do this that broke their model.

Even so, each snag taken on its own may not be crucial. Some shoppers like to shop one-stop and some don't. They could all fit in the big store at the same time. But the one-stop shop comes at a big cost – running cost. This can be the make or break issue in a sector with thin margins. Not only does it cost much more to run the big store compared to the small footprint store, but it's hard to change (see Topics 20 to 27).

If we assume they knew the precise route that had got them to where they are now, it would still take time and money to get back. It would be as if they had to start from scratch.

TOPIC 12 NOTES

[1] Lawrence Stevenson, Joseph Schlesinger, Michael Pearce, 'Power Retail' (Canada: McGraw-Hill Ryerson, 1999), 57-90.
[2] 'Shop fast and get out': See Note [3] Topic 8: David Walters & Jack Hanrahan, 'Retail Strategy' (UK: MacMillan Business, 2000), 253.
[3] Erich Gamma, Richard Helm, Ralph Johnson, John Vlissides, 'Design Patterns' (USA: Addison-Wesley, 1995), 24-5.

CHAPTER 3: SHOPPERS

Topic 13: Enter the dragon

IN THE CASE Study I compare the upstart, Illiad, with the leaders, Mastt. Mastt set and led the pace for many years. Mastt is a bunch of publicly owned UK companies (plcs), so anyone can buy their shares. Most of their shareholders are fund managers that invest in a range of companies. They all keep a close eye on the share price, and will switch into some other share if they don't like what they see.

Mastt is watched by their shoppers, their suppliers and each other. Each Mastt group knows what their rivals are doing. There has been no hint of price fixing, and no major price war. They have all played by unstated rules to get and keep their slice (share) of the pie (market).

Illiad was formed in Europe more than sixty years ago. They opened their first store in the UK thirty years ago. It's a private company and their shares are family owned. Thus they don't need to say in public what they are doing, and they don't need to pay dividends. They may choose to reinvest profits to grow their firm.

A firm that reinvests profits can grow faster than its rivals: it can open new stores more often. The more it grows the more it will be noticed. More shoppers may switch and start to shop with them. A tipping point is reached when rivals have to respond or lose more market share.

This point was reached in the Case Study in 2014. This is the same as in the real UK market, when the Small Two began to be seen as a threat to the Big Four. I use the same market share data in the Case Study as in the real world.

Sidebar

Some refer to the Small Two as hard discounters. IESE Business School gives a concise outline of the hard discount model [1]. The Small Two are German-owned firms. There are some sharp contrasts in the food retailing models of Germany and the UK [2].

TOPIC 13 NOTES

[1] See ieseinsight. com/ doc.aspx?id = 1125 and (on Aldi) at ieseinsight. com/ doc.aspx?id = 571 & ar = 14 & utm_ source = Web&utm_ medium = portal & utm_ campaign = Retailers_Aldi_ eng

[2] See economie.gouv. fr/ files/ files/ directions_ services/ dgccrf/ documentation/ dgccrf_eco/ english/ DGCCRF_eco22_Germany _ UK_food_retailing. pdf

Topic 14: Case Study: Mktg

EARLIER I GAVE a list of four keys to retail marketing in the 90s. Let's see how this relates to the firms in the Case Study at the present time. It sums up much of what we've looked at so far.

Mastt

Product range. Mastt shoppers have a choice from up to 40k lines or SKUs. There are some four brands for each product. This means that Mastt's 40k lines comprise some 10k distinct products. Half of Mastt's lines are store brands. The cost price of a store brand is up to a third less than the national brand of the same quality (see Topic 44). Their premium store brands are sold for a tad less than the national brands.

Their shoppers like the wide range. There may be a 'long tail' effect. This is where each product does few sales, yet where the sales of all products add up to a large amount [1]. It would be a risk for Mastt to trim their range of brands. They might lose sales from the long tail, as well as some of the shoppers who have come to count on it. For instance, if a shopper can't get the same wide range at the huge store on the edge of town they may switch to a rival shop close to home.

Shopper experience. Mastt has wide aisles for free flow. There is a sense of space, even at peak times. To the shopper there seems to be no limit to their choices.

Prices. Mastt's prices are low, but not the lowest. They have bargain offers, such as bogof, which change all the time.

Convenience. Mastt stores have good access and parking, even at peak times. With their large size and wide range, many of them are one-stop shops.

Recap: there has not been much change in twenty years from a shopper point of view, except it all looks bigger and better. They stock more store brands than they used to.

Illiad

Product range. They stock mostly store brands. The few national brands that they do stock tend to be household names. Their 1500 lines (SKUs) comprise some 1200 products. The shopper has less choice, so they choose fast; the store is small, so they shop fast. With its small range, the store needs less floor space.

Illiad's store brands are packaged as if they were national brands. There are entire product lines with the same name. Shoppers get used to these store brand names. In time, they come to see them as national brands.

Shopper experience. Illiad's stores and thus their parking areas are smaller than Mastt's. It's quick for a shopper to walk from their car to the shop and back. The shop entrance leads into the first aisle; it is a way to nudge shoppers into the funnel. Most of them take the same route. This means the aisles can be narrow. The shopper does not have so far to walk in a small store with narrow aisles. They fill their baskets fast because there are fewer choices. The cash till has large scanners, to speed up the transaction. Till staff have been trained to scan fast. Shoppers pack their bags after their goods have been through the checkout.

In all, then, for the same basket size, it takes a third less time to shop in an Illiad shop than in a Mastt shop.

Prices. These are classic EDLP. Illiad aims to be the lowest in the sector for the same type of product. It keeps prices low in two ways. One way is for their shoppers to shop fast: it means their stores can be small, so they spend less rent and wages for the same sales. This keeps their fixed costs low. The other way they keep prices low is that most of their lines are store brands: they cost a third less than national brands. This keeps their variable costs low (see Topics 20 to 24).

Convenience. Like Mastt their stores have good access and parking. But most of their stores are closer to where shoppers live. Stores are small so the parking zone is small: it takes less time for shoppers to walk to and from their cars. High street stores are close by, so shoppers can do top-ups after they have done their main Illiad shopping.

Illiad: Marketing aims

To give the best value at all price points. To stock store brands for higher gross margins. To pass on cost savings to shoppers. To open new stores out of past profits. To use standard layouts to speed up store roll-out.

Scope

To be the low-cost leader in basic groceries. To sell non-groceries as an impulse buy at cut prices. To focus on shoppers who like to shop fast and cheap.

Methods

Keep stores small, for fast shopping and low fixed costs.

Create a set of high profile and award winning store brands. Earn most of their sales from store brands, and not much from national brands. Search for costs to cut and pass on as lower prices to shoppers.

TOPIC 14 NOTES

[1] See en.wikipedia. org/ wiki/ Long_tail and en.wikipedia. org/ wiki/ The_Long_Tail_(book)

Topic 15: Johnny British: 1995

Illiad Case Study (fiction). Excerpt of a meeting between Illy and Homer in March 1995.

II: "Why do you think I engaged you?"

HG: "You like to have someone on tap with local knowledge who knows how you think. I can translate what you think into a British version. As you have said, you use people like me in other countries to do the same sort of thing. Gut-feel can be wrong; one can't rely on it all the time. So a mirror like me can be useful."

II: "Okay. First, help me deal with this problem that they seem to have in the UK with Jimmy Foreigner."

HG: "It's Johnny."

II: "Johnny! Of course yes! Okay, so is it a bad thing if they see us as foreign?"

HG: "For now, if your rivals think of you as Johnny Foreigner they won't see you as a threat. It's not hard for you to keep a low profile. They might catch on when your market share hits five per cent. Until then, they'll leave you to go your own way."

II: "Do you think it's a good thing that we are owner-run?"

HG: "Yes. You like to keep a low profile; that's a good idea for the time being. It gives you a chance to do things at your own pace. You don't need to hurry. It's not the same with plcs. Their bosses may not last more than five years, so it doesn't pay them to think far ahead. When you meet your next big goal you won't need to quit – you and your family firm will go on as usual."

II: "Is it a good thing if shoppers believe we just 'pile 'em high, and sell 'em cheap'? What about the myth that low price means low quality? If that's the way they think now, won't it be hard for them to change once we raise our profile? And won't it be worse if they see us as Johnny Foreigner?"

HG: "Once they shop with you a few times, they start to judge for themselves. Then they can ignore the critics. It's not as if groceries are fashion items. People buy them on price, as long as they meet their standards [1]. But I think you'll be safe to lie low for the next decade or two. With your plan you'll hit five per cent market share by then.

"Bear in mind that once you have a few hundred stores you'll be one of the most British stores in the UK. Shoppers and staff will all be British. Most of your suppliers will be British. You've said you'll use your profit to open new stores; it will all have come from British shoppers. Then they can call you Johnny British.

"Compare this to Mastt – they are all plcs. More than half of the shares of UK plcs are foreign-owned [2]. So most of Mastt's profits are paid to people outside the UK. In some ways those shareholders act more like punters than owners [3].

Looking ahead

"My last point is this. I agree that for those who don't know how it works it's hard to grasp that you can have high quality and low price at the same time. Give them time and they will get to know that that's what you do. In the next two decades you should aim to win every product award in sight. You should want this to be noticed. So you should go for premium quality products; and at festive times of the year."

II: "What about the class divide in the UK? Is it still there?"

HG: "What you and I think of as the demographics is still the main issue [4]. This can work in your favour. The market will find it hard to fit you into a type. That means that you should do well across all types.

"At some stage you won't want to be seen as just discount grocers. Until then your shoppers will come from the lower end of the income scale. You like shoppers to look at price and quality at the same time: then they can judge your products in terms of value for money. One way to get them to link price and value is for you to win awards. Then your shopper profile will start to stretch up and down the income scale. They will see your stores as the best place to buy groceries at the least cost, fast, and with no fuss."

II: "I like your idea that we should go for awards. That should cut across any class divide. Or, as you say, the demographics. We can think about doing that in ten years or so. No need to hurry."

HG: "Fine but, right now, I think you should stock a range of high-priced food items. If not, you won't see the high income shopper in the stores at all. The key is to sell luxury groceries at EDLP like you do with the rest. At some stage shoppers will see that you are the low-cost leader. The high income groups will buy more of your standard lines. They may start to treat your exotic ready meals as basic goods. In time, they'll see that other goods that you stock can be judged in terms of value. They'll start to catch on to what the lower income groups have known all along."

II: "I'm not sure about ready meals in the high price range."

HG: "Ready meals are on the up. They will soon be seen as essentials in all income groups. People work hard. They like to watch other people do things. They watch food shows on TV; then they grab a meal from the fridge or deep freeze. It's the same with sport: most people don't play but like to watch."

II: "The move back to ready meals may be part of a trend. It may take our group a few years to change. We'll stay with our range as long as we can, but I take your point about the demographics. One day we may have to do it.

"The shopper may think that some of our stock is exotic. Just because it's foreign. But from our point of view, we sell it off the shelf just like any other goods. So we don't need to charge a premium price. We go for our standard margins, yet to the shopper it is a real bargain."

HG: "Yes, I've seen your rivals charge a high price for goods that they import. As you don't pad your margins, your price may be half what they charge. You must be pleased when you see them do that sort of thing.

"The other point is trust. I think that it needs time to grow. People don't like to feel that they are being manipulated. Even in a small way. Transparency is the key to trust. Real EDLP – no bluffs – is the key. It's your best weapon. You are the low-cost leader. You want shoppers to catch on that there can be only one, and that you're it.

"But while it's best to be open with your shoppers, it's not the same with your rivals. With them, it's best for you to use stealth. You are going to disrupt their market at some stage (see Topic 31). So it's right that you should hone the way you do things before you go upmarket."

II: "Fine. We don't have the same snags with our shoppers in Europe. Maybe they just know who we are. I agree that when we get close to five per cent market share we should stock high-priced food.

More Q and A

"Do you have any questions at this stage?"

HG: "You don't seem to set much store by primary shoppers? Those who do more than half their grocery shopping at one store?"

II: "Mastt treats them as their main target and keeps track of them. They may think they are the same as loyal shoppers. But we don't think they are. We don't go out of our way to get them.

"We just want to be the first store on the shopping run. We give shoppers the best prices. They can get all the basics and quite a few of the extras. Then they can go and shop where they please. They save so much time in our store that their total shopping time may be less than if they had only gone to a Mastt store.

"Also, the kind of shopper who is set to split their shopping likes to pay less. That's why they come to us first. We call them the why-pay-more shopper. Not everyone is like that. We like them to compare prices. We don't have to look hard for that kind of shopper: they find us. We just need to be there, easy to find. Then we must get out of their way and let them get on with it."

HG: "I suppose shoppers can split their trips into small chunks to free up their weekends. They don't need to be slaves to the shopping expedition. But do you think that 20pc of shoppers are of the why-pay-more type?"

II: "In the rest of Europe it's at least 20pc. In tough times it may be more. But we take a long-term view. It's what we want come rain or shine. We're from Europe. We know that we could lose what we have at any time. It could be at the hands of a new rival as hungry as we used to be. So we like to lie low."

HG: "It would help if I knew what it is you like about this line of work? As a grocer, I mean."

II: "Trading gave me a buzz from when I was twelve years old. It's like when you talk to someone and find out that you each have a spare item that the other wants. Before too long you each walk away with more than when you met. It works like magic. That's retail: you give them an item, they give you cash, and you're both better off. Once I found that out I was hooked. I learnt that to keep shoppers coming back just make sure that they also win."

HG: "Fine. Next question: were you surprised to find out about Little's Law [5]? Did it prove that what you had been doing was right? Once you got to know the maths, did it help you to improve the way you do things?"

II: "I didn't need to know any maths to know that shopping speed was the key. I didn't need to know any maths to see how floor space and fast shopping time were linked. We do things based on what works in the stores, not on theory. But the maths is easy to work with. And it's nice to know that the maths guys are not too far behind the curve."

TOPIC 15 NOTES

[1] 36% of shoppers rate price as the most important factor when choosing products; 18% of shoppers rate quality as the next most important factor: gov. uk/ government/ uploads/ system/ uploads/ attachment_ data/ file/ 526395 / food pocket book-2015 update-26may16. pdf
[2] Owen Jones, 'The Establishment, and how they get away with it' (UK: Penguin Random House, 2015), 231.
[3] Charles Handy, 'The Empty Raincoat' (UK: Arrow Books, 1995/1994, Hutchinson), 149: 'Owners or Punters?'
[4] See getbrandwise. com/ branding-blog/ bid/ 18617/ What-are-marketing-demographics
[5] See web.mit. edu/ sgraves/ www/ papers/ Little's %20 Law-Published. pdf.

Topic 16: Customers: 1995

ILLIAD CASE STUDY (fiction). Excerpt of a meeting between Illy and Homer in May 1995.

II: "We once spoke about Mastt's strong points and how they could turn into weak points. Can we discuss that?"

HG: "Yes. You and your rivals have opposite points of view about the retail trade. Yours is old-school: sell basic goods at the lowest price. Focus more on the type of products that you sell than on the type of shopper who buys them. Treat all shoppers in the same way. You don't mind who they are, as long as they buy your goods. So you are product-orientated. I think we can say that it's the traditional view.

"Mastt's focus is on the type of shopper who buys their goods. Who are they, what, why, where and when do they buy? Mastt gears their product mix to the needs of the shopper, as a whole person. So they are market-orientated [1]. Here we are in the year 1995. I think we can say that theirs is the modern view. What do you say to that?"

II: "That's right. But they stress the brand and the image of the brand. That strikes me as too much like above the line advertising; it sells the brand and the experience. Retail should focus on below the line advertising; one should stress the product and its price. At least, it should be that way when it comes to basic goods.

"They say the retail shopper is loyal to the brand. That's fine for fashion goods. But, in the long term, with basic goods, you have to focus on price and value. Our rivals share with us the view that the shopper is king and queen. We just focus on the product price and value because we found it's the best way for us to look after the king and queen."

HG: "Your rivals' scope may be too broad to do what you do. On the one hand they sell basic groceries; sure, that should be all about price and the product. On the other hand they want to lure the shopper in, to spend more time in the store. To do that Mastt has to provide a wide range of non-basic goods. This is in the hope that shoppers are tempted to browse. It's more about the brand and the experience. The risk is that they send mixed signals."

II: "How do you think it came about?"

Origins

HG: "Because of IT, firms can now deal with shoppers one-to-one. At the point of sale firms pick up all the data about brands sold. Their loyalty card data tells them what brands each shopper bought. Their systems can match the two. They can target offers to their shoppers more than they can with bogofs. It costs less. And they get a good response.

"Mastt talks about share of shopper rather than share of market. They want to sell their shoppers more than just basic goods. So they stock a wide enough range of products to serve most needs. When they broaden their product range they enlarge their scope. It does two things. First, they can sell a wider range to their own shoppers. Second, it brings new shoppers into their net. It is why they speak of economies of scope as well as of scale [2].

"This is fine as long as long-term repeat business is part of the deal. When you buy a car, you keep going back to have it serviced; you might buy the same brand next time. Or, when you buy a mobile phone you sign a contract. If they want to keep your custom it makes sense for retailers to think in terms of brand loyalty.

"But if you buy a tube of toothpaste for £2, that's the end of it. You sign no contract; you don't need to have the tube of toothpaste serviced. When you run out you might see the same brand on offer somewhere else for £1. You'll buy it if you need it then. You don't have to wait until you're in your home store.

"In broad terms, Mastt's way works best when shoppers' needs differ a lot. Like when they buy books: there are heaps of titles to choose from [3]. Reader's tastes differ a lot. So bookstores need to stock a huge range. In your case shoppers buy groceries. But their needs don't differ that much. Also, Mastt's way works best when the amount spent by each shopper differs a lot. Like how much each person spends on flying: some fly now and then; others go abroad all the time [4]. But when shoppers just buy groceries, how much they spend does not differ that much. So, both ways, Mastt's way wouldn't work so well for the lines that you sell."

II: "I agree that it's hard for Mastt to build brand loyalty on the back of basic groceries. A repeat buy might not be a sign of a loyal shopper. If they are in a big store, and it stocks their toothpaste, they'll buy it. But I thought you were so keen on the rapport with shoppers? That you think it's the key to repeat deals?"

HG: "No, sure, you're right. Despite what I've said, I think that Mastt still has the momentum. They should make a lot of money doing it this way for many years. At least until their rivals are all doing the same thing.

"But I also think it's quite subtle. Illiad wants the shopper to trust that their prices are the lowest. Not just for basics but for all goods. Trust is the residue of a good deal, and it grows by accretion. The more they trust you, the more likely they'll come back. The way you have built up repeat business has been through transparency. EDLP gives a strong message – your store is the brand."

II: "Fine, Homer. There's a good case for both views. What they are doing works for now.

"The battle is always the same when one deals in basic goods. It's not a case of winner takes all; we each get a fair slice of the pie. We think that when the dust clears our slice should be at least twenty per cent. We just want Mastt to come to terms with that."

TOPIC 16 NOTES

[1] See also en.wikipedia. org/ wiki/ Marketing
[2] See also en.wikipedia. org/ wiki/ Economies_ of_ scope; and see people.hofstra. edu/ geotrans/ eng/ ch2en/ conc2en/ economies_ types
[3] Don Peppers and Martha Rogers, 'Enterprise One-to-One' (London: Piatkus, 1998), 56.
[4] See Note [3] above, 59.

Topic 17: The flip side: 1995

ILLIAD CASE STUDY (fiction). Excerpt of a meeting between Illy and Homer in May 1995.

II: "Why should we care how Mastt sees things?"

HG: "The way their top people see the market shapes the kind of decisions they make. People shop in one of your stores when they want to buy basics. When they want to buy fashion items they go to other shops. But you don't care when or where they shop for fashion. Mastt does care about things like that.

"Mastt knows their shoppers in the round, the whole person. They want to cater for all their states of mind. So they offer them goods across a wide spectrum. It's why they believe in the one-stop shop."

II: "Maybe this is Mastt's way to defend their choice to go for big stores far from the centre? Once the shopper is captive, they can be sold the kitchen sink. Which came first, to go for big stores, or to serve all shopping moods?"

HG: "One thing led to the next. They wanted big stores to give them economies of scale; it would raise their fixed costs but that would be fine if they could sell in volume – then they could cream it.

"To boost volume they thought they should sell more than just groceries. That led them to stock a wider range of goods. They would have gone for those with high gross margins. The rest followed from there. They have a few store types and sizes, to suit diverse shopping moods. Out of town stores are for big trips; those in the city centre are for quick visits. The idea is that the shopper stays with their store group because they trust the brand. All the pieces fit in a neat pattern."

II: "That's okay so far. How does it relate to me?"

HG: "We should compare their bogof with your EDLP. Some say that bogof is one of the great inventions of the last century. It's like a free hit of dopamine for the shopper. And it's what Mastt is best at. We all know that EDLP is boring. Yet EDLP is made for comfort; we feel a quiet sense of triumph when we walk out of that store having saved forty quid. That's what you give them. So both bogofs and EDLP have their plus sides."

Not always good

II: "But there may be a dark side to bogofs?"

HG: "It's a gamble. You may get a bogof on your choice brand of coffee, or maybe not. It might be next week. Gamblers don't mind losing a bit each time, but now and then they must have a fix. They go for a bogof. But it's like a roulette wheel."

II: "Okay. Let's compare that with the key benefit of EDLP. If the shopper trusts that the EDLP price is almost always the lowest, their trust in our brand goes up. If they trust us on one thing, they might trust us on the next thing.

"Whereas with bogof they don't know what the price of that product used to be. Do you think that they think that the price they see now could be a con?"

HG: "Perhaps. They may feel that's it's all a game of who outwits who. That the deck is stacked in Mastt's favour – the only ones who know the value of the hidden cards. Mastt knows what they paid for the coffee;

they may peg that price too high for a few weeks; then the new price can look like a bargain. But the shopper may start to distrust the message. They may become less keen on the game if they think it's rigged in Mastt's favour. Even if it's not rigged.

"The shopper does not get that dopamine hit with Illiad. But they do know that they save cash each time they shop.

"Mastt runs the risk that at some point the shopper will start to think 'who pays for all this? Me?' I think that the Aladdin's Cave effect works well for now. The shopper sees all this profusion and feels pampered. The aisles are wide and there is a great expanse of colour and lights. They see it as the peak of shopping in the twentieth century. Mastt hopes to lull the shopper to spend more. Once they buy a small luxury they might spend more on groceries.

"But what happens when every store group is doing the same? Will the cave still look so exciting to the shopper? Or will their feet be too tired?

"Despite the snags, your rivals have a great strategy. Yet so have you. Both groups can find the kind of shopper that suits them. You just want to find your kind of shopper; that's why it makes sense for you to seem to be so different from Mastt."

II: "I think I know when shoppers tire of bogofs. It's once they find that they save much more from one shop with us than from a bunch of bogofs from Mastt!

"We would lose our edge if we moved to bogofs. It would wreck the way we work out our gross margins. As you know, we have a standard gross margin for each category. If a supplier drops their price, we pass most of it on to our shoppers: thus our margin stays the same. In that way, all of us – staff and suppliers – are forced to focus on sales. Not on squeezing out more profit from a smart bogof deal. For us, the big snag with bogof is that it steers one's eye to the profit on each item; the right way is to look at the sales: profits follow."

HG: "Fine. I think I know why, but tell me why would you not want your staff or supplier to squeeze out the most profit from each bogof?"

II: "Our staff would have to be smart all the time to get the most profit from each bogof. Yet that wastes time. Standard margins are easy and quick to use. The smartest people at head office are better used to source good deals for shoppers.

"Also, the shopper wouldn't like it if they thought we were trying to outwit them. Now what they see when we cut a price on an item is the new lower price. Not some offer that makes them buy more in order to get it."

Update

In 2016, at least one store group cut down on bogofs [1].

TOPIC 17 NOTES

[1] See Topic 47, Note [3]: dailymail.co. uk/ news/ article-3442252/ Sainsbury-s-supermarket-axe-bogof-deals-research-confusing-shoppers-actually-spend-1-274-year

Topic 18: Aim for mood: 2015

ILLIAD CASE STUDY (fiction). Excerpt of a meeting between Illy and Homer in March 2015.

HG: "Why do you aim for the mood and not the person?"

II: "As you said, Mastt aims for the whole person. That is, they try to deal with all their diverse moods. A person gets into the right mood to shop for groceries; it may be once a week or so. From time to time they are in the mood to shop for a basic good that they need, like an appliance. In other moods the person may shop for leisure goods. Mastt tries to serve all these moods from one big destination store.

"But the snag as we see it is that people might not want to mix these shopping moods. When they shop for groceries, they want to get in, buy and get out. So the first way we differ from Mastt is that we cater for only this mood. On the way they might spot an impulse bargain, but we'll ignore that for now.

"All types of people are in the mood to buy groceries at some stage. That's why we don't need a clear profile for each type of person to work out what they want and when. We just say, whoever you are, when you're in the mood to shop for groceries, here we are. We've got what you want, at the best price, so you only need to come here when it suits you. In this way, all types of people should feel at home when they shop with us.

"There are lots of spin-offs in doing it this way. Note that Mastt looks at the ways in which people differ, while we look at the ways in which they are the same. So it's harder for them to keep it simple. We don't need to be all things to all people. We're one thing to all people. In one fell swoop we get rid of the need for hundreds of staff at head office. We don't need them to work out all the things that diverse types of shoppers might want at various times. And this is the same no matter how big we grow. We just replicate a small store many times. We think that one of the secrets of how to scale – to grow big and fast with no strain – is to stay with the same structure. One also sees this on the internet.

"As soon as we see that there's more than one way to do something, we choose the simplest way. We try to do the right things over and over; and to do it better, inch by inch. We might not see the gains straight away. Yet now and then some of these simple ways act in tandem; that's when we see big gains all at once. In some ways it's like the way the British cycling team trained for the last two Games."

HG: "Is this the same with your shops in other countries?"

II: "Not as much as you might think. We've learnt from the UK. In the 90s, in other countries, they spoke about UK supermarkets in hushed tones. Mastt was known to be ahead of the game. But in a way Mastt had too much success for too long. They kept the same old model well past its sell-by date.

"Yet we've come to realise a few new things – through your input and what we've found at our UK stores. It's that we don't need to be the same thing to all shoppers at all times."

HG: "For instance?"

II: "We now have a whole range of exotic foods and ready meals. Only a small share of our shoppers buys these lines. But for them it's now a regular thing. And they see these lines as essentials. It does mean we have to stock a wider range. All our new stores are a bit bigger than the old ones. Yet we don't need the stores to be twice the size, as you know. Shoppers who may have come in to buy one or two exotics now buy most of their groceries from us. This adds up to more sales per shopper, per store, per square metre, per month.

"We can do all of this and yet still stick with our core approach. We are fine as long as we are the cheapest at any given level."

HG: "Do you plan to export this way of doing things to your stores in other countries?"

II: "We'll see. We know our stores mustn't get too big or we'll lose our fast shopping edge."

Topic 19: Impulsion: 1996

ILLIAD CASE STUDY (fiction). Excerpt of a meeting between Illy and Homer in May 1996.

II: "We know that shopping for basics can be boring. Fast and cheap shopping helps, but it might not be a cure for boring. We do add a bit of zing with our specials. These are first-come first-served goods on sale each week. No one knows what they'll be until the last minute. Shoppers buy things on impulse that they didn't know they wanted.

"One reason our stores can be small is that each week we stock only a few impulse goods. We limit our stocks, so that they are sold out in a week or two. We do it to tip the balance, for shoppers to come back each week."

HG: "Aren't these the same sort of goods as those stocked by Mastt as standard?"

II: "Yes. It's one reason their stores have to be so large. Mastt faces a few big snags. They have a lot of online rivals who stock these goods as standard. Online may be cheaper. And, when the shopper knows what they want, online is quicker.

"We like to include 'must buys' for the home but we don't stock them as standard. People don't buy them often. They know what they want when they see it. And they know their prices. We get good prices – suppliers know we'll sell them all and sell them fast. We pass those prices on to shoppers; that is, we just take our standard margins. We know that shoppers don't forget where they bought their bargains."

HG: "How much of your stock consists of impulse lines? Are they just sweeteners?"

II: "It's close to a tenth of our sales so for us they are not just sweeteners. Shoppers might not find an impulse item every time. But on most weeks they'll find one. The bargain price may tip the balance.

"It's the place where many of our shoppers 'discover' an item that they want. But we don't try to catch them with the idea; we prefer to catch their eye. They don't have to think; they can just grab.

"The internet may not be the best place to look if you don't know what you want, or if you have only a vague need. It is fine for 'search', but less so for 'discover' [1]."

HG: "It is harder to predict the sales of impulse lines than it is for groceries. At least when you run out of an impulse line, shoppers won't blame you. They'll blame themselves for not being there that week. I bet you it works the other way at Mastt stores – if they run out, shoppers are bound to blame the store!

"Most of all, I like it that you might stock as many lines as Mastt does; you just don't do it all at the same time."

TOPIC 19 NOTES

[1] See also mashable. com/ 2011/ 09/ 06/ browsing-content-discovery/ # dTXH7gBTkZqo

CHAPTER 4: MARGINS

Topic 20: Whose profit?

FOR A FIRM to do well in the long term it's best to have feedback about how it's doing at each step. To get that, managers need to start with some kind of plan so they can check it along the way.

Feedback is clearest when it's in the form of numbers. This is where accounting comes in. Its main job is to keep score; as part of that it has to produce numbers. But when these numbers are used to help run the firm, accounting is more than just keeping score.

In retail, most of the key numbers come from the profit and loss account. The chief of these relates to gross margins. We look at this in the next few topics.

But before I start on gross margins, I'd like to take a quick detour on the subject of finance. This has as much to do with the balance sheet as the profit and loss account.

When they set its financial policy, managers of a firm decide on three things.

The first is to decide where it gets its capital. It can get some from its owners and the rest can be borrowed. The former is known as equity, and the latter as debt. The big choice to make is how much of each.

The second thing is to decide how it is going to invest its capital. This is where they weigh up the 're-turn on investment' for each project they look at.

The third thing is to decide what it does with its

profit each year. They decide how much should be kept in the firm. Much of it may be used to grow the firm. What's left might be paid out as dividends to share-holders.

Now we can look at how this might work in practice.

Let's say it's the end of the year and the Illiad bosses have to decide what to do with its profit. They have three main options, which they can mix and match.

The first is for it to pay tax on its profit and to pay out the rest as dividends to the owners. Let's say that its owners don't need dividends. So they cross this option off their list.

The second is to pay the tax on the profit and keep the rest in the firm to open new stores. They put this option on the shortlist. We can call it 'jam tomorrow.'

Their third option is to give the profit to the shopper now. How? The firm doesn't take the profit in the first place. It gives it away to shoppers in the form of lower prices. The firm adds this option to the shortlist. We can call it 'jam today.'

Which of the two options on the shortlist should they choose? From a strategic point of view?

Is there a combo choice? That is, give some of it to shoppers in the form of lower prices, pay the tax on what's left over, and keep what's left in the firm to open new stores? They might even save some of the tax when they open new stores. Let's say they want to give just enough discount to shoppers that their rivals can match. Rivals won't go bust – they just won't have spare cash for growth. That would leave the way clear for Illiad to pick and choose where and when they want to grow.

This is not just a numbers game. Illiad would not mind what Mastt does in response. But they would mind what their own shoppers want. So they would first look at the effects of each choice on their shoppers. It may be that the combo strategy is best. Some jam today, some jam tomorrow. Shoppers score now; and the firm still grows. Lower prices push up demand; more stores pushes up supply. Today's slice and tomorrow's cake both get bigger.

Sidebar

Who gets the jam? It has to be the shopper. As the aim of a business is to create and keep a customer [1], it's best to give them the jam. Both today and tomorrow.

TOPIC 20 NOTES

[1] Peter Drucker. See Topic 11, Note [2].

Topic 21: Accounting talk

IN TOPIC 6 I gave a list of some of the accounting words I use in this book. They all come from the 'profit and loss account', which is a list of sales and costs over a period of time. I repeat that list below. I use the words on the left, not those in brackets on the right. Money is in GBP; sales exclude VAT.

- Sales (aka turnover, revenue)

- Cost of sales (aka cost of goods sold)

- Gross profit: 'GP' (sales minus cost of sales)

- Running costs (aka operating expenses)

- Operating profit ('GP' minus running costs)

The list continues with a few other items that we don't use much: these are shown below. Run your eye down the words on the left on both lists. Apart from the top line (Sales), each line is either the name of a type of cost or of a type of profit. In each case we subtract a cost from the profit above it to arrive at a new profit. Thus profit is always what is 'left over'. What dictates the next profit item on the list is the type of cost that gives rise to it.

This is important, but why? Why don't we just have three items: Sales, Costs and Net Profit? Why don't we skip the bits in between? The answer is that each pair of 'cost-profit' items tells its own story. In this book we need only look at two stories, that is, two types of cost. Once we are clear about what these two costs mean, we'll know how their cost structure works. Then we can spill the whole grocery stores' can of beans.

Here are the other items on the list, those that we hardly use in this book.

- Non-operating costs (non-operating expenses)

- Profit before interest and tax (aka PBIT; EBIT)

- Interest and tax (aka Finance costs and tax)

- Net profit (PBIT minus interest and tax)*

  * aka net income

I'll now write a few words about the first list. Note that we start with Sales. Below Sales is the first cost we want to know about. It's the Cost of those sales, which we subtract to get the Gross profit.

Cost of sales is paid mainly to suppliers for goods. The store calls these goods 'stock' and puts them on their shelves to sell to shoppers. There are other costs of sales which we can ignore here.

The next costs are those to run the firm – running costs. They include wages, rent, logistics and power. We subtract them from gross profit to get the operating profit.

We now have two types of cost and two kinds of profit. These two types of cost don't work in the same way. Cost of sales depends on how many items the store sells. If they sell twice as many, the cost of sales will be twice as much. But the store also incurs running costs over a period of time. These costs stay more or less the same no matter how many items they sell in that time.

These two types of cost are the main ones used in this book. They are basic to retail firms and many other kinds of firm. Later on we'll see that the way the Big Four deal with these costs may affect how well they solve their problems.

Note that there are two other types of cost and profit that play no real role in this book. But I will describe one of these costs briefly. A non-operating cost is one that is neither a cost of sales nor a running cost. Let's say that a store revalues one of its properties. Say it is now valued at less than what is shown in the balance sheet: this means that there has been a loss, that is, a 'cost'. But that cost does not fall within the firm's main line of work, which is to buy and sell goods. So they don't call it a running cost. Instead, they call it a 'non-operating cost'; then, when they subtract it from operating profit, they are left with the third type of profit (PBIT). In short, they take this cost out of 'running costs' and put it elsewhere. As this type of cost plays no part in the job of being a grocer we won't need it until later, when we look at property and share price.

There are two more crucial items to add to the list that we will use. They are to do with the word 'margin'. Margin means 'profit as a percentage of sales.' As we have seen there are four types of profit, which means there are four types of margin. In this book we just need to know about the first two types, 'gross margin' and 'operating margin'. These two types of margin play a crucial role in this book; I look at them in the next few topics after this one.

As I've said, each type of profit tells its own story. We tell the story up to the end of 'operating profit'. This means that we will only need to use the first five items in the list. I look at them, along with margins, in the next few topics.

A retail firm does not make things, so it does not need big machines. This is why in this book I focus on the profit and loss account, not on the balance sheet. It is what retailers should do, but much of the time they don't. They might buy a range of assets that they wrongly think will 'strengthen' their balance sheet. Then they get in a muddle when things go wrong.

Topic 22: Margin magic

WE CAN USE 'margins' to turn dull accounting data into all but magic. Let's say we buy and sell a product – floor rugs – for a profit. I'll start with the links between the selling price, the number of items sold, and the profit.

Say we sell one rug for ten pounds. That gives us sales of ten pounds. If a rug costs us four pounds then our cost of sales is four pounds. Our gross profit is sales less cost of sales which gives us six pounds.

If we work out the gross profit as a percentage of the selling price we get the gross margin. Six as a percentage of ten – the selling price – is sixty per cent. Good. Sixty per cent! Superb.

So far we've looked at it per rug. We can also work it out in terms of total rugs sold by, say, the end of the day or month. We add up the sales of all the rugs to get the total sales. Then we add up the cost of all the rugs sold to get the total cost of sales. Subtract the two to get the total gross profit. The gross margin is the gross profit stated as a percentage of sales. It is worked out in the same way whether we look at it per rug or for all rugs.

Say we sell a thousand rugs this month. Our sales, cost of sales, and gross profit are all a thousand times as much as they are for selling one rug. But what's our gross margin? Sixty per cent! No change. No matter how many or few rugs we sell, our gross margin is still sixty per cent.

That's the start of the magic. The gross margin can be relied on to be more or less constant no matter how many or how few items we sell. So what is magic about margins? We'll take it one step at a time as we move through the topics in this chapter. The first step is just to know that when we use the word margin it always means a percentage. Always. And it should always be a percentage of sales.

At some time in the past you might have worked out how much something costs to make or buy. Then you might have added a mark-up to work out a selling price. That way of working it out is called cost-plus or mark-up. When you start to think in terms of margins you'll need to put aside cost-plus or mark-up, for now at least.

In private you may want to translate margins back into cost-plus or mark-up each time. At some stage you may see how easy margins are to work with and to compare with other firms. Then you might choose to stick with margins and drop cost-plus and mark-up.

Say we want to work out at what price we should sell a rug. If we were working with cost-plus, we might start with what the item cost us and then work from there. On the other hand, when we work with margins, we start with how much we think we could sell the item for. Then we work backwards. So we start with our estimate of the selling price and subtract what it cost us. This gives us our gross profit – and it might be zero.

What do we do if our gross profit looks like being zero or less? Then it's back to the drawing board. Buy it for less or look for something else to sell. But don't think we can solve it by changing our selling price. The selling price is what we think we could sell an item for.

That doesn't change just because our costs look too high. Selling price is decided by the market, by what's out there, by the price of other similar products. That's when we find that margins help us the most; they too are based on the selling price.

Say we wanted to start a new firm that sells rugs. We would like to know a bit about the cost structure of that type of firm. In the same way, say we already had a firm and wanted to sell a new product, such as rugs. We would like to know about the cost structure of that type of product. It's best to work it out before we start.

There are two key things we should know about the typical cost structure of any type of product. The first is the selling price and the second is the gross margin. If we find out that our cost of sales would be too high to get the typical gross margin then we have a problem. We have to solve it before we leap into the new venture.

For instance, say we find out that the typical gross margin that rival shops make from our kind of rug is 80pc, not 60pc. What does this mean? A gross margin of 80pc means a cost of sales of 20pc. That tells us that those shops pay about two pounds per rug. That's half of what we thought we'd have to pay. So that's the real problem. We still have to solve it but at least we know what it is we have to solve. We have to find a regular source of supply of these rugs at two pounds each, not four. Before we go into this venture.

Of course, most firms are not going to tell us their gross margins, or even the gross margins in that sector. But there are ways to find out. We could start with friends and family. They might know someone who

knows. Or we could try an accountant or business broker. Or if we want to find out for nothing – just for our
time – we'd use the internet.

So far I've made no mention of running costs.
They don't come into it at this stage. In retail 'we live
and die by our gross margin.' Sort that out and we are
nearly there. Until we sort it out we're nowhere at all.
That's why, before we start to look at supermarkets, we
need to know about their gross margins.

Topic 23: Margin secrets

AT THE END of this topic, I hope that readers can say 'if Mastt tries to keep up discounts of 6pc they'll go bust'. Readers won't need to check with the official experts. By then they should know more about how to work with prices and sales, and what these do to profits.

What is the gross margin in supermarkets? What are the gross margins, I should say. There is a range of gross margins. It depends on the type of product. Is it fresh? What is its storage cost? How long will it last? In each case the gross margin is based on a ton of factors. The simplest way to start is to manage products by category. These may be groceries, dairy, frozen, produce, floral, meat, deli, bakery, and general. Each has its own usual gross margin. Firms can then drill right down to the level of each product.

But firms won't tell you their gross margins. It's like a state secret. They'll explain, 'it depends'. But they know precisely: their firm lives and dies by their gross margins. Each month or week or day, by category, product, store, you name it, they know their gross margins. They not only know their own, they may also know those of their rivals, to the decimal point.

Have you seen their gross margins in print? No? What they mean when they talk about their margin is likely to be their operating margin.

Recall that our sales are ten thousand pounds for the thousand rugs we sold. And our gross profit at 60pc gross margin is six thousand pounds.

We now need to work out our operating profit

(OP). To do so, we deduct our running costs. These are rent, wages, power, and logistics and so on. Let's say they are more or less the same each month. In our case, if running costs for the month are five thousand five hundred pounds then our OP this month must be five hundred pounds.

Now we can work out our operating margin. That's OP as a percentage of sales. Five hundred is 5pc of ten thousand.

To recap: gross margin is 60pc and operating margin is 5pc. What can you do with gross margin that you can't do with operating margin? You can treat gross margin as a more or less fixed percentage of sales. But you can't do that with operating margin.

OP and thus operating margin depend partly on running costs. These costs relate to how the firm is run as a whole, not to the sales of each product.

You might sell twice as many products, and make twice as much gross profit, and yet have no change in running costs. Your gross margin would still be 60pc, but OP and thus operating margin would go up sharply. So your operating margin does depend on how much you sell. But it does not do so in proportion to sales.

What does operating margin tell us? It tells us more or less nothing about how a firm runs its business. As the 'bottom line' it tells us that they made a profit, but not how they got there. What we'd like to know is their gross profit, their gross margin and, only then, each item of running cost. That would tell us more about how they run their business. The firm's operating margin is like the punch-line to a story. How it gets from gross margin to operating margin is like the story.

We want to know the story.

Take two firms from different sectors. You and I each own one of the firms. Each firm may have an operating margin of five per cent yet have got there by different routes. Let's say that both firms had sales of one hundred pounds for the month. This means that both firms earned five pounds OP.

Let's say that your firm's gross profit was sixty pounds and my firm's was ten pounds. This means that your gross margin was sixty per cent and mine was ten per cent. (The first clue that the two firms are not in the same sector is that their gross margins aren't the same).

We both ended up with five pounds OP. Your running costs must have been sixty minus five equals fifty five pounds. My running costs must have been ten minus five equals five pounds. So the OP of these firms is the same yet their cost structure differs a lot. That's the start of why we need to know about gross margins.

In what way does this link to supermarkets?

No more suspense

It's time to get rid of the suspense. Let's say that the usual supermarket aims for a gross margin of some 27pc. That's what I use in my workings.

This is not about rules. Just rules of thumb. Once you've used rules of thumb to find out how a thing works you can always plug real numbers back into your workings. Once you know the real numbers.

Often you find that you don't need to be too precise. You are still able to get a real feel for how the numbers relate to each other. That is the case here. Recall that I wrote earlier that soon you'll be saying 'if

Mastt tries to keep up discounts of 6pc they'll go bust'. Can you say that yet? Just read on.

Say that Mastt's sales are £100k. At the usual gross margin, gross profit is £27k. We don't know what their running costs are since they won't tell us. But say they tell us their operating margin is 5pc (of £100k); that means their OP must be £5k. If we reckon that their gross profit is £27k, then their running costs must be £22k, being £27k minus £5k.

What happens now if they give their shoppers a discount of 6pc? That means their sales drop to £94k. What is their cost of sales?

We must take care here. To start with, we assume that they sell the same volume of goods and that they pay the same cost price as they did before. At sales of £100k, less gross profit of £27k, cost of sales would have been £73k. After we give our discount, cost of sales would still be £73k.

Let's recap. Sales £94k less cost of sales £73k equals gross profit of £21k; less £22k running costs, oops. That's an OP of minus £1k. How long can they last? When will they run out of cash?

You may say we should have taken a short-cut. We should have gone straight to the old OP of £5k and subtracted the discount of £6k to get the £1k loss. There was no need for us to know a thing about their gross margins. We could have done it even more quickly, by saying, look, they told us their operating margin is 5pc. So if they give away a 6pc discount then, straight off, they have to be minus 1pc, which is a £1k loss.

That's true, but I wanted to take you the long way round. It'll come in useful later.

Topic 24: Margin games

PERCENTAGES CAN BE fiddly to work with. Say we want to convert an amount to a percentage. We should first state what we want to compare it to: that is, the amount that we want to stand for 100pc.

Let's take it from where we left off in the last topic.

What was their old gross margin? Their old sales were £100k and their old gross profit was £27k. Thus their old gross margin was 27 as a percentage of 100, or 27pc. It should be clear that in this case we want £100k to stand for 100pc.

What is their new gross margin? Their new sales are £94k. Their new gross profit is £21k. The new gross margin is 21 as a percentage of 94, or 22pc. That's a long way down from 27pc. It should be clear that in this case we want £94k to stand for 100pc.

Let's try to answer this one: what was the percentage change?

Well, we can see that the gross margin (percentage) has changed. By how much has the gross profit (amount) changed? That is, how does the change in the margin, a percentage, affect the profit, in pounds?

Two numbers have changed here. Gross margin has changed and gross profit has changed. So we have two questions to answer, not one. We must work out how much the gross margin has changed, in percentage terms, compared to what it was. And we must work out how much the gross profit has changed, in percentage terms, compared to what it was.

Gross margin was 27pc and is now 22pc. Can we say that our gross margin has dropped by five per cent? After all, 27 minus 22 is 5? It depends on what we want to know.

Say we want to get a feel for how much our gross margin fell. We must compare both the 'before' (27pc) and the 'after' (22pc) to 100. Then we can subtract them and say that 'our gross margin fell by five percentage points', just like we said above.

But we might want to know by how much our gross profit fell. We want £27k to stand for 100pc. That means we must compare both the 'before' (£27k) and the 'after' (£21k) to £27k. We subtract them, to get 6; then we compare 6 to 27, not to 100. Let's repeat that – 'compare 6 to 27, not to 100'. We work out that 6 is 22pc of 27. In this case we would say 'our gross profit fell by twenty two per cent.' That's by more than a fifth.

It might help to say it in words. Our selling price dropped by just five per cent. Yet our gross profit dropped by twenty two per cent. That is quite striking. It shows how a small discount can trash the gross profit.

Why do these two ways differ? In the first case we said that 'gross margin fell' and in the second case we said that 'gross profit fell.' The 'margin' is a percentage; the 'profit' is a sum of money.

To make sure that we don't get muddled we could write the amounts in one column and the percentages in the next column. We should always write 100pc next to the amount at the top, being the amount we want to compare it to.

Here's the trick, the one sure way to get it right.

We know it isn't deep science but basic arithmetic. We can invent many examples, like those above; then practise using them, over and over. That's the only one sure way I know to get it right.

We've seen that Mastt can't afford to give more than 5pc discount unless they can find out ways to recoup it. The discount is quite easy to work out. The hard part is to find out ways a store can recoup it. Stores have three ways to recoup a discount from their trading. Sales can go up. Cost of sales can go down. Running costs can go down. In practice, these ways are used in combo. We'll look at them in the next three topics. Then it should start to become clear what Mastt — and the Big Four — are up against.

Topic 25: Push up sales?

WE CAN USE trial and error to work out by how much sales need to go up to pay for discounts. We can start with where we were in the last topic. Sales were £100k. Operating profit before discounts was £5k. If we gave £6k in discounts and nothing else changed then we would make a loss of £1k. Our new gross profit would be £21k and our new gross margin would be 22pc.

Now we can refine the question. 'If we give discounts of 6pc by how much would our sales need to go up for us to make the same gross profit as before?'

We should first work out what the new gross profit would have to be. From that we can work backwards to find out what the new sales would have to be. We know that the new gross profit needs to be £27k, the same as it was before any discount. We know that our new gross margin is 22pc.

Now that we have some numbers we can refine the question some more. 'If we give discounts of 6pc by what percentage would our sales need to go up for us to make £27k gross profit at our new gross margin of 22pc?'

(It would help here if we convert our gross margin to a ratio. To do this, we divide 22 by 100 and get 0.22.)

To work out the answer to our question we should divide the gross profit we want to have by the new gross margin ratio. We divide 27 by 0.22, which gives us 123. So shoppers would need to spend £123k. They now spend £94k. Thus they would need to spend

£29k more than they spend now. The extra £29k is 31pc of £94k.

Thus: 'if we give discounts of 6pc our sales would need to go up by 31pc for us to make £27k gross profit at our new gross margin of 22pc.'

It seems like a high price to pay for what seems to be a feeble discount. To pay for a discount of 6pc, sales would have to go up by nearly a third! Why is this so? And how likely is it that a market leader could boost sales by that much? We can now check how this would work in the Case Study.

Let's say that we don't think that the size of the cake – the market – is getting bigger. And let's say that Illiad gives 'discounts' of no more than six per cent. We know that Mastt can't match this. So they could not take market share from Illiad. Mastt would have to take market share from their rivals, the other Mastt groups. But don't they, too, give discounts? Would we not just see a price war between all the Mastt firms, where they all lose? While Illiad would just grow as they did before?

We can sum up some of the learning points from this topic.

The first is that even a small discount can cause a huge fall in operating profit. This is due to the cost structure of the sector. Low margins means that there's not much room to play with discounts. We could say that in a low margin business you need a huge increase in sales to cover the cost of small discounts.

The next point is that the market doesn't respond to discounts as fast as we might think. My guess has been that in the real world it'll take up to six years for the Small Two to take away a sixth of the sales of the Big Four. And, even then, most of their gains will come from opening new stores (see Sidebar below).

We could say that the total gain to shoppers who each get a small discount is far less than the pain to the store group that gives it.

The third point is that when market leaders make a fuss about discounts it might be aimed at their own shoppers. They want to convince them not to desert. Shoppers might be all set to believe that their usual store will match the prices of rivals. If so, then they might say, 'why bother to try out the rest?' It may be too kind for us to say that the leaders make a fuss about discounts just to calm the fears of their shoppers. But if that's not why they make a fuss, one may presume, it's because they don't know that such discounts won't save them.

Sidebar

At the start I compared the growth rate of the Small Two to that of the Big Four. Then I worked out how many stores the Small Two would need to get a market share of 20pc; and then how long it would take. I went on from there. What their rivals might do did not come into it. Rivals are locked in to what they do at the time. They would only start to react if they thought they might go bust, and it would still take years for them to respond in full. That's where I think they are now.

Topic 26: Cut costs?

COULD MASTT CUT costs to pay for discounts that they give to shoppers?

As we have seen, there are two types of costs. Running costs do not go up or down in line with sales. It's cost of sales that go up or down in line with sales. These two types of cost differ so much that we should look at them one by one. I'll start with running costs. As they don't change much in line with sales they are known as fixed costs.

By how much would running costs need to fall for Mastt to make the same gross profit as they did before they gave 6pc discount?

We can work this out without a calculator. At present say they make £5k operating profit (OP) on sales of £100k. If they give discounts of £6k then their running costs would also have to fall by £6k. That would bring their OP back to £5k. That's easy to work out. But how likely is it?

We know that total running costs are some 22pc of sales. Based on my figures (see Topic 34), Mastt's labour costs are 10pc of sales. This means that, for sales of £100k, labour costs are £10k. They would have to more than halve these costs to pay for discounts of £6k. But how could their giving discounts help them to cut their labour costs? These two items aren't linked. One would expect that by now they would have brought labour costs down as far as they can. We can use the same logic to work out that they can't cut their rent, or asset expenses.

Thus Mastt can't expect to cut fixed costs to pay for discounts.

Now I'll look at cost of sales. These costs are called variable, as they do go up and down in line with sales. By how much would cost of sales need to fall for them to make the same gross profit as they did before they gave 6pc discount?

If we gave £6k discount our new sales would be £94k. Our cost of sales is £73k at present. Our new cost of sales would have to fall to £67k for us to recoup £6k. How likely is it that suppliers would give back £6k of the £73k they get now? By now, surely they would have cut prices to Mastt by as much as they can? What makes us think that they have room to cut their prices to Mastt by an extra 9pc?

There are two cases to look at.

The first case is if it is a national brand. Would a supplier take a risk and cut prices for just one of the Mastt firms? What would the other Mastt firms have to say? Would a supplier risk losing the custom from the other Mastt firms? Would they be willing to cut the size or quality of their product? The answer to all of these has to be no.

Yet if suppliers did the same thing for all of the Mastt firms the market share of each would stay the same. No change. So the answer to the main question has to be no. A supplier would not cut the prices of their national brands to suit one of the Mastt firms.

This brings us to the second case, that of store brands. Let's say that as things stand about half of Mastt's sales come from store brands. They may now wish to bump up their use of store brands, and cut their use of national brands. This would cut their cost of sales because they pay less for store brands. They may work as partners with their suppliers to change the design and prices of these brands; in this case, none of their rivals would have a say. Each store brand differs from those of all their rivals. It is their way of being different. And, as they can't be the cost leaders, they have to differ from the rest to stay in business (see Chapter 5: Frameworks).

So one of the routes they can follow is to move more into store brands. But it's overkill: it's too big a change just to pay for discounts. It's more to do with their broad strategy of how to be different from their rivals. The snag is that this won't happen fast. It could take a Mastt firm a few years to devise and carry out such a new broad strategy.

I'll sum up this topic. For Mastt to cut their costs so that they can afford to give six per cent discount they would have to change the way they run their business. Even at six per cent they would be running on empty. More than that would make it worse. To change the way they run their business will take them a few years even if they get it right.

Topic 27: Swap FC with VC?

BY LAW, FIRMS have to draw up their financial statements in more or less the same way. It also gives those who deal with the firm some idea about its size and nature.

But managers in a firm need to know about the numbers in more depth. They aim to run their firm better. They arrange the same data in a new way, to get to what they call their management accounts. This data does not have to be made public.

Earlier, I wrote how the two main kinds of costs differ. Costs that go up and down in line with sales are called 'variable costs' (VC). Cost of sales is a variable cost. Costs that are more or less fixed for a period of time are called 'fixed costs' (FC). Most running costs are fixed costs.

Cost of sales includes all costs to get the goods on the shelves ready to sell, such as inward freight charges.

Some running costs act more like variable costs – and not like fixed costs – in that they go up and down in line with sales. Yet these costs don't form part of the cost of sales. For instance, credit card fees are only incurred at point of sale, when the shopper pays for the goods. The fees can't be rolled in with cost of sales as they were not part of the cost to get the goods onto the shelves. Thus card fees form part of a new group, called 'other variable costs'; they need to be taken out of running costs.

These two types of costs are split in the management accounts (see Sidebar below). Managers need to know which costs are fixed and which are variable when they work out prices.

This is not being too fussy. We know that each percentage point counts in retail. It's vital for managers to keep tabs on which of their costs are variable and which are fixed. Say sales goes up by ten per cent and there is no change in fixed costs. By how much will operating profit go up? It depends on their gross margin. It's no good to just guess or cross fingers.

When there are just a few shoppers in the store, managers try to cut fixed costs. If they can't, they try to find ways to switch fixed costs to variable costs. This is good for the shopper as well as for the store and their staff. It means that stores can stretch or shrink their running costs more in line with sales. For instance, when the store is nearly empty they can run it with a skeleton staff. They may cross-train their staff, who can then change roles on the fly. Or else, when the store is nearly full they can top up with temp staff. This means that some of their wages will be variable costs.

The effect is that the store can stay open for more hours in the month for less cost and still make a profit. It results in more options for the shopper and more hours for staff to work and be paid. The aim is not to have precise data for the sake of it. It is to keep tabs on how their costs act and change over time. Retail stores know this. They know how to manage their costs, and how to switch them from fixed to variable.

But the Big Four may need to refine and extend the way that they do it.

The Small Two have made of it a fine art. Their great skill has not been in piling stock high and selling it cheap. It has been in managing their fixed costs. It's not easy even though they make it look that way. It's not easy to copy, as I'm sure their rivals are finding out. It goes to the heart of how their firms are run.

Some small retail chains on the high street – such as the pound stores – do the same sort of thing. Big retailers can't ignore it. It is one end of the wedge that will change the structure of the retail market. The other end of the wedge is of course the internet.

These last three topics have looked at ways for stores to recoup the cost of shopper discounts. There are not that many. Too few to get smug about. In Chapter 5 (Frameworks) we can once again take a broad view.

Sidebar

A firm splits their costs along these lines in their management accounts. They would have 'gross profit' less 'other variable costs' to get a second type of gross profit, called 'contribution'. It's used in the same way as 'gross profit'. We don't need it in the rest of this book, so we'll stick with 'gross profit.' But readers who want to use it in practice may wish to look it up [1].

TOPIC 27 NOTES

[1] See en.wikipedia. org/ wiki/ Contribution   margin

CHAPTER 5: FRAMEWORKS

Topic 28: Strategy

I FIRST LOOKED at the state of this sector late in 2014. I checked for signs of change in market share for each of the main store groups. That's when I spotted that the Small Two were steaming ahead, right under the noses of the Big Four.

Then I did some workings based on what I thought their gross margins were likely to be. As I don't know their actual margins I did it on a 'what if' basis. The main aim was to check how sensitive profit is to a change in sales and prices, and to see which small causes have the most impact.

This is all much as I described earlier in this book.

But the whole time, the fact that the Big Four can't seem to stop the Small Two from taking their market share lurked in the back of my mind. Over the years I've shopped with all six store groups. I've observed the way they worked. I've noticed that the Small Two and Big Four differ a lot. All they seem to have in common is that they both sell groceries.

At some stage I thought that shopping speed might be the key. But it took me a while to grasp that it was an ideal fit for Little's Law [1]. This can show the impact of speed on flow rate. I had to look at flow rate in more depth. But first I had to grasp why the market as a whole seemed to have missed four key points.

One: the two groups of firms do things in a very different way. **Two:** for years the market share of the Small Two has gone up fast while that of the Big Four has stayed the same or shrunk. **Three:** point One seems to have been the cause of point Two. **Four:** if the Big Four don't make big changes, things will go on in the same way, and for the same reasons.

To grasp why they had missed these points I needed to know more about what each of these store groups did, and in what ways they differed. Then I could compare them. Only then would I try to answer the question: why do the Big Four still seem to be so baffled by the challenge?

In one sense, the root cause can always be found in how a firm does what they do. There are a few ways to describe what a firm does. For instance: 'the way they do things'; 'their business model'; or just 'their strategy'. I worked out what the strategies of these groups might have been in the nineties. That's when most of them were put in place (see Chapter 2: Background).

I've found it's useful to use known 'frameworks' to think about the strategy of a firm. It helps to spot if it shows a pattern that was used in the past. A framework is more help than a checklist. It's like a checklist with a structure. There are scores of frameworks to choose from. Most of them are described as a theory or a model or suchlike, but I treat them all in the same way. I don't use them to find deep truths or prove something. Instead, I use them to help gain insight into what goes on in the firm or sector, which is what we want to do here. Or to gain insight to solve a problem, like these firms no doubt want to do.

A framework is not a theory and it can't be proved. It's a set of guidelines, with rules of thumb, not rules. It's quick to check if the framework seems to 'fit' the current case or not. It's easy to discard if it doesn't seem to fit. There's no need to waste time in blind alleys.

It's fine if a framework fits only part of the problem. To solve part of it may be a good way to gain ground [2].

There can be at least two broad aims when managers try to solve a problem or manage a firm. One is to be 'efficient' and the other is to be 'effective'. Drucker wrote that the first is 'doing things right', and the second is 'doing the right things' [3]. In one sense, the first may have to do with 'ops mgmt', when they look inward, to the firm; and the second may have to do with marketing, when they looks outwards, to the market.

Managers first need to work out the most effective path, or else they may land up doing the wrong thing well. It's the key to marketing. Once they're on the right path they can try to be more efficient in the way they do things, by doing them over and over; and by trying to do them better all the time. That's the key to ops mgmt.

It seems that twenty years ago the Big Four came up with an effective strategy. In some ways it made them the envy of the retail world. As time passed they grew more efficient in how they carried it out. Yet they might not have been so effective in giving shoppers what they wanted. It does not matter how right they did things if they stopped being the right things.

Twenty years ago the Small Two also came up

with an effective strategy. They too were efficient in the way they carried it out. Yet as time has passed it's still effective. It's kept pace with shoppers' changing needs. That may be why the Small Two have got as far as they have.

In the next few topics I describe some of these frameworks and how I applied them to the store groups. The aim was to work out what sort of bind the Big Four had got into, and if there are ways for them to get out of it.

TOPIC 28 NOTES

[1] See en.wikipedia. org/ wiki/ Little%27s_law
[2] See also G. Polya, 'How to Solve It' (UK: Penguin, 1990/1945), 157-60: 'Progress and achievement.'
[3] Peter F Drucker, 'The Practice of Management' (Oxford: Routledge, 2011/1955).

Topic 29: Decide on scope

THIS IS ONE of the first issues that managers of a firm should decide on.

It's not enough for them to say what they want the firm to do: what its aims are. They should also say what they don't want it to do. That means they need to decide on its scope: it sets limits to the aims.

Thus the firms we discuss in this book are in the 'retail' business. But they are not in all types of retail. Their scope is not as broad as that. Say that you drew a large circle and called it 'retail'. You could draw a small circle inside the large one and call it 'supermarkets'.

To start with we can say that the scope of the Big Four is all more or less the same. But the Small Two sell a smaller range of products than the Big Four. We can say that the scope of what the Small Two do is smaller.

Firms can define scope solely in terms of the product range, as we do above. That is, in terms of 'what' they sell. They can also define it in terms of the type of shopper, or 'who' they sell to. The type of shopper they would like to sell to is called their target market. They may have more than one target market.

Then they can define it in terms of the market in which they trade. That is, in terms of 'where' they sell their product. This may be the place where their store is located; it may also be the market 'space' in which they sell, and who their rivals are.

These are three of the main elements of scope – what, who and where. Some people call it product-market scope. But we can stick with scope.

We can classify each of the six firms in terms of their scope. We should keep this in mind for later, when we look at what's gone wrong for the Big Four and how they might fix it.

These thoughts about scope have been around for some time. Then in the 1980s Michael Porter came up with a bunch of new thoughts of his own [1]. If modern strategy could be said to be like an airport, Porter built the runways. I am going to touch on one or two of his ideas. He used the phrase 'generic strategies' to describe in broad terms what paths a firm has to choose from [2]. Here is my shortcut to work it out for any firm. There are three steps in the process.

The first is to work out its scope. We decide if the firm serves the whole industry, or just a segment (slice) of it. If it serves all segments we can say that its scope is 'industry-wide.' To start with, let's say that that was the scope of all of the Big Four. We could put all of them into a big circle called 'supermarkets'. Note that all four are in the same circle.

If a firm does not serve the whole industry, then it means that it serves a segment. We should not be surprised that they call this 'focused.' We might say that the scope of the Small Two is focused on 'supermarkets: basic groceries.' This could be shown as a small circle inside the big one.

So, at the start, the scope of each of the Big Four firms was industry-wide; and that of both of the Small Two firms was focused on one segment. That's the first step in the process. All we need to do is put each firm in one of our two circles.

The next step is to work out which firm is the

low-cost leader in their segment. There can be only one in each segment. Now, which of the Big Four is the low-cost leader in the big circle, supermarkets? That is, which one seems to always have the lowest prices? Let's say that you think it is X. You may say, well, they always talk about EDLP and you've shopped there from time to time, so you think that they're it. Or you may choose Y, on the grounds that they claim to match or beat the prices of the other three. You choose.

Now for the third and last step. The low-cost leader differs from the rest in that it is the cheapest. Each of the other three of the Big Four has to differ from the rest in their own way. They can't be the low-cost leader as there can be only one of these in each segment. You may want to work out all the ways the other three differ from each other.

That's the end of a shortcut to work out the generic strategy of any firm.

It may seem to be too simple. Surely it can't just boil down to answers to the three questions: 'in what segment is the firm? Is it the low-cost leader in that segment? If not, how does it differ from rivals in its segment?' The short answer is, yes, it does just boil down to that.

But a firm may differ from its rivals in more than one way. Each of these ways describes a point of difference. You should choose how much weight to attach to each point. Then, scope can change. Top managers in each firm must decide what its scope is now and what they would like it to be. They need to keep it up to date. The process needs to be ongoing. So they can never rest and say they've nailed it down now and forever. The main thing for them is to draw a line between the markets and products that they intend to focus on and those that they don't.

Once you're clear about scope, the rest follows in common sense sequence.

Sidebar

I defined scope in broad terms. Say store A sells stoves and store B doesn't. Are both still in the same segment? If not, could they each be the low-cost leader in their own segment? The key is how the shopper sees it.

Say that store A starts to sell building materials. How wide can scope go before the store is no longer seen to be in the same segment as the rest? How viable is such a hybrid approach?

A store may serve a number of needs and a number of market segments. It may help to define the scope of each. In this book we don't need that level of detail so we define scope in broad terms. We focus on those stores that shoppers see as 'supermarkets.' For this reason, I've assumed that shoppers see the Big Four and the Small Two as more or less part of the same segment.

TOPIC 29 NOTES

[1] *Michael E Porter, 'The Competitive Strategy' (NY: Free Press, 2004/ 1980); and 'Competitive Advantage' (NY: Free Press, 2004/ 1985); and see hbs. edu/ faculty/ Pages/ profile.aspx? facId= 6532*
[2] *See also ifm.eng.cam.ac. uk/ research/ dstools/ porters-generic-competitive-strategies*

Topic 30: Points of difference

THIS IS ONE of the topics where we need to use some of the jargon. But not for long. Once we translate it into plain words we can drop the jargon again.

In the previous topic we looked at how the managers of a firm decide on its strategy. They choose its scope, that is, the segment in which they want it to trade. They work out if their firm is able to be the low-cost leader and, if so, if they want it to be. If not, they have to decide how it will differ from its rivals.

They say that if you can't be the cheapest, be different. This is not the same as being better. Yet it's not enough for the firm to just differ from its rivals. Their target market has to like it.

Let's say there are four newsagents in the town centre. Say you own one of them and you move it closer to where your customers live. Your shop is now in a different location from the rest. Do your customers like it? If the answer is yes, your sales and market share should rise. You differ from your rivals in a way that your target market likes. It is called a competitive advantage [1]. Or, we could say, you have an edge.

If rivals move next door to your shop, what happens? Then your edge is lost. But if they can't move close by – perhaps because of zoning laws – then your edge is said to be sustainable [2]. Or, we could say, you keep your edge.

So it helps to get an edge on your rivals, but the main thing is to keep it.

If you get an edge, you gain market share. If your

rivals can't match you, you'll keep your edge and your new market share. Every firm is always on the lookout for this: to differ from the rest in a way that can't be matched. What if your rivals are quick to match what you do? Then you no longer differ from them. You have an edge until you lose it. If they can match you then they can catch you, and you go back to your old market share.

It does not seem to have been too hard for rival stores in the Big Four to match each other. It's hard for a firm that sells basic groceries to differ much from their rivals. The key word is 'basic.' This is not the case with other types of retail firms. In the world of fashion it might not be as hard to look and to be different.

Here are some examples of points of difference in supermarkets.

Free advice on how to use the product. A hundred per cent refund on goods, for a month after they were bought. Loyalty card points that can be used to buy goods at your stores. And at other stores. A food outlet in the store. Banking facilities. (Do these look quite flimsy? How hard are they to match? Enough to get an edge? For how long can they keep it?)

As long as a firm exists they have to address the issue of how they differ from the rest, what edge that gives them, and how they intend to keep it.

They can also differ in many ways: a bit here and a bit there. If you have the corner shop, that may be an edge. If it's on the high ground, that may be an edge. If your customers like it and your rivals can't match it then you might keep your edge. An edge helps you to stay in business.

In the mid-90s, the Big Four began to extend their scope. Their product range was now more than just groceries. It went outside what this sector had sold before. In Topic 12 I wrote how IT helped to make it happen. It started with a leader: they led the way and the rest tried to catch up. It's fine to be the leader, until they all catch up and have the same strategy.

Now, twenty years later, things have changed once more.

In the eyes of grocery shoppers, the Big Four might have begun to look the same. The ways in which they differ are not enough. And what they now offer may not be quite what shoppers want. By now the Small Two have grown big enough to be noticed. They have the edge in a way that shoppers like and rivals can't match. Cheap! Quick! Small! Close by! They are now taking big chunks of market share from the Big Four.

This seems to be about where the market is now. The wave that swelled up over the years has begun to break.

TOPIC 30 NOTES

[1] See also en.wikipedia. org/ wiki/ Competitive_ advantage
[2] See also hbr. org/ 1986/ 09/ sustainable-advantage

Topic 31: Being disruptive

NOW AND THEN someone invents a new framework that changes the way things are thought about. In the 90s Clayton Christensen [1] came up with one. He showed how a new firm in an industry, one that starts at the low end, can push top firms out of the market. A few years later he called it 'disruptive innovation' [2].

This phrase – both words used in concert – has been used so often that it's now a cliché. But it's so useful that it's sure to have a long life. I'll describe a shortcut way to use it.

First, some background. Joseph Schumpeter [3] came up with the phrase 'creative destruction' [4] in the thirties. It stands for how, in capitalism, the new drives out the old. Since then, this phrase has been one of the most quoted in economics. But there are snags if you try to use it in business.

A good strategy framework helps us to learn how things work and to solve new problems.

It's hard to use the phrase 'creative destruction' to work out why the PC drove out the mainframe. And it's hard to use it to work out how a new firm can thrive in the grocery sector. But we can use 'disruptive innovation' to do both. Thus it may be one of the most useful frameworks ever. Here is how I would sum up the way the phrase 'disruptive innovation' can be used.

Say our firm is new to a market. We launch a cheap version of a proven product. The quality of our version is so poor that customers who use the proven product don't want ours. Our price is too low for us to make a fair profit. Yet there are still some people who buy our version. They can't afford the proven product but prefer ours to none. So there is now a new market segment that buys our poor version at the low price.

It may be best for those who make the proven product to stay out of this segment. Thus they should not bring out a low cost product of their own. Their profit would be too low. The low quality might harm their core brand. It would seem to make more sense for them to leave this segment to us.

The next step for us would be to use our profit to ramp up the quality of our next version. Low as this profit might be. Those customers who buy it may have more income than those who bought our first version. Yet they still can't afford to buy the proven product.

We go on in this way, step by step. Each time it makes more sense for those who make the proven product to stay out of the new cheap market. And for the same reasons. Each time we ramp up the quality of our product. At some stage we ramp it up to the stand-ard liked by customers of the proven product. As our price is lower, they switch. The makers of the proven product may have to leave the market.

The key is for us to keep ramping up the quality, and to keep the price down. To do this, we have to in-novate. Profits can come later.

That's my shortcut view of the framework. The web is crammed with examples. Most of the new ver-sions are small, fast and cheap. They range from cars and phones to disk drives and fuel cells.

We can use a framework to gain insight. In the mind's eye we place it next to the new problem and, if it fits, use it. If not, we move to the next framework. This one seems to be a good fit for the UK grocery market. It doesn't mean to say that one or more of the Big Four will need to leave the market. But they'll need to make room for the Small Two to move in next to them.

Sidebar

Schumpeter was an economist so he gave a broad macro view. His phrase is too abstract to help solve business problems. It calls to mind the word 'revolution'; it may be what commerce looks like from the outside, looking in. It's also quite broad; it could apply to 'the known universe and all that is in it', not just to capitalism.

The words used in Christensen's phrase are less grand, but they do help to solve problems. His phrase calls to mind the word 'evolution'; it is a micro view of what commerce looks like from the inside, looking out.

The word 'disrupt' harks back to the word 'erupt': it can come up from below. It's also more like words such as 'disturb' and 'displace'. None of these words bring to mind the word 'destroy'. In commerce, the new does not 'destroy' the old. PCs did not destroy mainframes, but they did disrupt the market for systems. When PCs took over, some firms that had made mainframes – such as IBM – weren't 'destroyed'. They adapted and have since thrived.

Change in the ways of trade tends to evolve. The guardians of the old hold on as long as they can. This may be a good thing. It might not stop the change but it gives people more time to adapt. This is not a new idea. It is how evolution has managed to work for so long. Natural selection does not invent from scratch but builds on what it can use from the past [5].

The word 'create' suggests something made from scratch. The word 'innovate' suggests that something is changed. More firms innovate than create. HotBot search preceded Google. MySpace preceded Facebook. The phone and the computer preceded the internet.

This is why 'disruptive innovation' seems to fit more with how change takes place in commerce. It changes things that are there at the time; it disrupts but does not destroy what was done before. It's more like a race than a boxing match. Old ways that don't change aren't knocked out: they just fall behind and fade away.

When Christensen first set out his views he used the word 'technology', but later he changed it to 'innovation'. This moved his framework from being just about the technical into the mainstream of strategy. It shows why the costs of products fall over time; why it is rare for the market leaders to be the ones to lead the change; and how a free market can evolve.

TOPIC 31 NOTES

[1] See hbs. edu/ faculty/ Pages/ profile.aspx? facId= 6437 and claytonchristensen. com/ key-concepts
[2] The Economist, 'Disruptive technology/innovation', 11th May 2009: economist. com/ node/ 13636558
[3] See en.wikipedia. org/ wiki/ Joseph_Schumpeter
[4] See en.wikipedia. org/ wiki/ Creative_destruction
[5] Dario Maestripieri, 'Games Primates Play' (NY: Basic Books, 2012).

Topic 32: Using frameworks

HERE ARE FIVE steps we can use to check if a framework can help to solve a new problem.

Step One. Gauge if at first sight the framework is a good 'fit' to the new problem.

Step Two. Check out a past problem where the framework was a good fit.

Step Three. Judge how well the past solution solved the past problem.

Step Four. Use the past solution as a guide to solve the new problem. Keep in mind where the old and new problems differ. One may choose to use only part of the past solution.

Step Five. If it still fits, add it to our list of viable ways to solve the new problem.

Here's how we can use the five steps to test the phrase 'disruptive innovation'.

Step One. On the face of it this framework is a good fit for the sector. The Big Four chose not to compete with the Small Two on the lines of 'keep it small, speed it up'. It left the Small Two free to grow to more than a thousand stores. Until the banking crash in 2008, the Small Two might have focused more on low income groups. Since then their shoppers seem to be from all income groups. This shows that the Small Two must have started to ramp up their game.

Step Two. Personal computers (PCs) posed a threat to IBM's market power in the eighties. IBM thought they could thwart the threat if they had their own PC firm. But they knew that their own PC firm could not have the same cost structure as that of their mainframe firm; and they would also have to sell to a brand new set of customers.

Step Three. IBM formed a new PC firm with its own cost structure and marketing arm [1]. This approach worked well for years.

Step Four. In the same way, a Big Four firm could start a new chain of small footprint grocery stores.

The snag is that the new problem differs from the old one in at least three ways.

One. The Big Four would need a few hundred stores at good sites to make a dent in the Small Two's market share. This may take years. This issue – the need to scale up fast – was not a snag for IBM. It sold mainly through dealers.

Two. The grocery sector has too much floor space – demand is less than supply. It was the reverse with the early PC market – demand was more than supply. Thus it may be too much of a risk for the Big Four to add yet more floor space.

Three. The markets for PCs and mainframes were not the same. A person who paid a few hundred pounds for a PC could not afford to buy a mainframe for a few million pounds. So there was no threat (in the first few years) that PCs would take sales from the mainframe market.

In contrast, the target markets for both old and new Big Four stores would be the same. They would all be grocery shoppers. Shoppers at their large stores might switch to their new small footprint stores. The large stores would lose sales. So a chain of small Big

Four stores might cannibalise sales of their main brand.

It is true that some of the firms in the Big Four have their own convenience stores [2]. They might have thought to change them to a new small format. In that case they would not need to open new stores. It would mean they could scale up fast; and they would replace, not add, to total floor space in the sector. But the small store could still cannibalise sales of their main brand. Also, a good site for a convenience store may not be a good site for a small footprint store.

A new brand with a new name would face these same snags.

Thus the snags faced by the Big Four are not the same as those faced by IBM in the PC market.

At least the test shows we can use a framework in another sector, time and place to cast light on new problems. It throws up some of the issues faced by the Big Four that we might not have thought of. For instance, the need to think about how to scale up fast; the current state of demand and supply in the sector; the chance to draw new shoppers; and the risk of losing current shoppers. It is the start of what should turn out to be our in-depth checklist.

The use of a framework can help in other ways: it can act as a trigger for new ideas. The old and new problems can be put side by side and used to generate new thoughts [3].

It can be used to hone the way the question is phrased. It seems to me that in some cases the best question is a spec of what we want from the answer; the problem statement lists the conditions that the solution must fulfil. But it may be hard to list them all at the start of the task. Solving this kind of problem is a design process. We imagine what we want and try to work back to where we are; or we start with what we know and work forward to where we want to be. A bit of both may be best: we can start at either end.

To recap: it looks like the Big Four are being disrupted by the Small Two. To think of ways for the Big Four to address this, we looked at one case (the IBM PC) from three decades ago. We walked through what they did at that time, but found that their solution might not work with the new problem. We also dug up a few new things that a solution needs to include.

We could go on in this way and use the framework to check out other past problems and how they were solved. Even where we don't solve the new problem, it can help us to tease out some of its features. In this book I've just stuck to the one framework. But we could try the same tack with other ones.

TOPIC 32 NOTES

[1] See thocp.net/ biographies/ estridge_don
[2] See also en.wikipedia.org/ wiki/ Tesco
[3] 'The old and new...' see: Steven Pinker, 'The Stuff of Thought' (UK: Allen Lane, 2007), Ch. 5.

Topic 33: Implementing: 1995

ILLIAD CASE STUDY (fiction). Excerpt of a meeting between Illy and Homer in June 1995.

HG: "How do you make sure that your plans are carried out in the way you'd like?"

II: "We don't have much in the way of grand plans. We think long-term but actions take place in the short-term. We use constant feedback to make sure that plans are carried out.

"A retail store is about as simple as one can get. Buy cheap and sell dear. Our structure is no more complex than the things we have to do. For each sixty stores or so we have one regional centre to serve them. Stores and regions each need their own type of manager. We don't need other levels between them. This structure lets us turn head office rules of thumb into quick action in the stores.

"We do most things in a standard way. Our structure then backs up these standards. For instance, we have just three store sizes; they all have the same procedures. It makes it easy to compare stores. A lot of store managers can report to one manager at the next level. It makes training quick and easy – to train for one store is to train for all stores.

"We don't pin mission statements to a wall. We talk about what we want done using plain words that we all know. It's to make sure that a message doesn't get twisted on the way up or down.

"At the top we give rules and guidelines. Ideas about better ways to do things can come from the stores and bubble up. They are in the right place to do this because they know what makes the stores tick. That completes the loop."

HG: "Do you get them to compete?"

II: "We do, but each store is treated as a team. Within stores, peer rivalry pushes people to try harder; they do that to keep up with the rest of their team. It helps to keep out free riders.

"Then we can compare how well each store is doing. This rivalry between stores makes sure that people don't get too big for their boots. It helps to keep out the bullies.

"We use a mix of incentives, for teams – in the stores – and individuals. We place far more weight on teams. Our best stores run as tightly-knit teams. So rivalry in the firm is mild to warm, not hot.

"We have expert staff at head office and the regions to manage the data. They have to match supply and demand at all of our stores. We spend huge sums on IT."

CHAPTER 6: SECRETS

Topic 34: Unpack the mantra

IT'S OFTEN SAID that what the Small Two do is to 'pile 'em high and sell 'em cheap.' I think it's more correct to say that they 'keep it small and speed it up.'

The old mantra might have been useful up to late in the last century. But by then real-time IT systems had helped to slash stock levels. The need to keep a big pile of stock fell away. The new challenge, led by the Small Two, is to speed things up and use less space.

I recap in brief how this new mantra works and then flesh it out later on. The new mantra has a double whammy.

'Speed it up' refers to how fast shoppers pass through the store. It is measured by how long they take to shop, from entrance to exit. The less time they take the more sales and hence gross profit the store can make per square metre of floor space per hour at peak times.

The store may keep the extra gross profit. Or they may choose to cut prices. This would be a way to pass on the extra gross profit to shoppers as a discount. This should bring in more shoppers. Grocery shoppers like to pay less and they like to get in and out fast (see Topic 7).

Either way, if they can 'speed it up' the Small Two should make more gross profit at peak times. It is the first whammy faced by the Big Four.

'Keep it small' refers to the size of the store and the number of staff. These two items account for most of the running costs of a store. With small stores, these costs should be less.

Thus if they can 'keep it small' the Small Two should make more operating profit (OP) per GBP of gross profit at all times. It is the second whammy faced by the Big Four.

To sum up, if they speed up shopping they can afford to cut their gross margins. If they keep the store small they can cut their running costs.

We may ask which comes first. We could say that the answer is 'keep it small.' This is because it lets them do two things, not one. First, all stock on the shelves is close by. It's quick for the shopper to find and helps to speed up shopping. Second, it's quick for the shelf stacker to reach, and it cuts down on rent and wages. This brings down running costs.

Or we could say that 'speed it up' comes first. The reason is that it is fast shopping which bumps up the hourly sales and gross profit at peak times. If we look at it this way, fast shopping is the aim. 'Keep it small' is just one of the ways to achieve that. To keep it small is a method, not the aim.

Later, we'll come to why they need both. It's like one hand washing the other. The things a Small Two store does to 'speed it up' help to 'keep it small' and vice versa. To speed it up they have to get rid of bottlenecks and streamline the shopping process. This means they have to simplify.

And that's the next big secret. When they keep it simple, their running costs fall away like melting snow.

Sidebar

For Mastt's cost structure I use 27pc as their gross margin and 5pc as their operating margin. This leaves 22pc for their running costs.

I've said that Illiad can do the same sales in less floor space than Mastt. Thus their running costs should be less than 22pc.

What can we glean from the real world? What are the real costs and margins? Firms don't have to disclose this sort of data. But it is common knowledge to many of those who work in the sector. Those who know won't say. But the curious reader may be able to find out.

As I don't know what these costs are in the real world, I made them up for Mastt and Illiad. First I searched for some guidelines. In late 2014 the Wall Street Journal (WSJ) wrote about UK supermarket costs [1]. I used some of their data to make up costs to use in the Case Study. These may help the reader to narrow down the range to look for if they do their own search.

The main running costs are 'labour costs' and 'costs of fixed assets'. These are broad terms. I will refer to them as wages and rent. The rest of the running costs add up to a bit less than half of these two combined.

For Mastt, wages are 10pc, rent is 5pc and the rest is 7pc: that adds up to 22pc. For Illiad, wages are 7pc, rent is 3pc and the rest is 4pc: that adds up to 14pc. The two groups differ by 8pc.

This means that Illiad could give 8pc discount to shoppers, and yet make the same 5pc operating margin as Mastt. Or, if they gave no discount, it would leave them with an operating margin of 13pc. That's more than twice the OP of Mastt for the same sales.

These are the costs I use in the Case Study. If those in the real world come close, it would be clear that as things stand the market leaders can't compete on price.

In the next few topics I explain in more detail how and why the new mantra works.

TOPIC 34 NOTES

[1] See wsj. com/ articles/ diet-plan-wont-cut-it-for-u-k-supermarkets -1415897351. If you aren't a subscriber, you may be able to access the article by entering some of the keywords from its title into your search engine.

Topic 35: Why keep it small?

THIS TOPIC SHOWS how even though it has small stores Illiad can do better than Mastt. Let's say that at the start both groups have the same profile. That means they have the same sales, cost structure, operating profit (OP) and product lines; they are just as efficient; and their shoppers shop at the same speed.

Let's say that all at once Mastt makes their store twice the size. They are now able to get up to twice the sales and twice the gross profit at peak times. But the (fixed) running costs may be up to twice as much all of the time. The result is that – at best – their OP may be up to twice as much as Illiad's. For each store it depends on how many peak hours they have.

Let's look at the sector as a whole. If floor space goes up but there is no change in total sales, then the sales per square metre will fall. Mastt's sales as a group should fall, and it could get worse if floor space in the sector keeps on going up.

Now let's look at it per store. Say that the new Mastt store is never more than half full. That means there are no peak times. If the same number of shoppers wants to shop at Illiad, then Illiad would never be full. Both stores could land up with the same sales and gross profit. But Illiad's fixed costs are lower, so they would make more OP than Mastt. Even if demand were too low for Mastt to break even, Illiad might still make some OP.

How low can they both go? They both need some shoppers to cover their fixed costs (and so break even).

Illiad has half the fixed costs of Mastt, so they need half as many shoppers to pay for their fixed costs. Thus if there is too much floor space in the sector, the smaller store has more chance of breaking even.

To recap, in tough times a small store is more likely to survive than its big rival. Why? It breaks even on fewer sales. In good times a big store is more likely to thrive than its small rival. Why? It has more floor space so it can make more OP at peak times.

Now we can look at it more closely. We want to work out when it's better to opt for the small store, and when to opt for the big one. We also want to work out why Illiad would opt for small stores in the first place.

Illiad is averse to risk. They use their own money and don't like debt. Instead of either-or, we should look at both-and. It may be that Illiad wants both the penny and the bun. This would be to avoid going bust in bad times and also to cash in on the good times.

How could they have the best of both? So far, they've done step one, which is to minimise their downside (by keeping it small). Now they can go on to step two, which is to maximise their upside (by speeding it up).

Remove the scaffolding

This is where we can start to relax our assumptions. Once they have helped us to grasp the main issues, we should be able to remove some or all of them, like scaffolding. In what ways could Illiad be more efficient than Mastt? There are at least two ways. One is if their shoppers shop more quickly. Two is if their fixed cost structure is lower. If a store can do the first then the second should follow.

At this stage we need not look at how Illiad shoppers could shop more quickly. To start with let's just assume that all at once they could shop at twice the speed. And that there was no change in Illiad's fixed costs. We know that Mastt has twice their floor space. What would happen?

Both stores could now serve the same number of shoppers per month. That is, they could have the same throughput. In that case, in the absence of discounts, each would have the same sales. But Illiad's fixed costs are less than Mastt's. So Illiad makes more OP than Mastt at any level of sales.

They do not even need to have only half the fixed costs for this to hold true.

It gets worse for Mastt as Illiad adds more stores. Floor space in the sector goes up. If total sales stay the same then sales per store go down. Even if Mastt's sales fall so much that they start to make a loss, Illiad might still make a profit.

So a lot rides on this small matter of shopping speed.

Is there a way out for Mastt? First, let's look once more at Illiad's OP when it goes for both small size and fast shopping. We know that they should make more OP than Mastt. But does this happen only at peak times? Is it only at peak times that the size of the store becomes an issue?

No and no. It is true that shopping speed only becomes an issue at peak times. But Illiad will make more OP all of the time because their fixed costs are lower all of the time.

At the same time, Mastt gear the size of their stores to what they expect at peak times. If they didn't do that, they'd forfeit sales and OP at those times. Peak times may be two, ten or twenty per cent or more of the hours that the store is open. But their fixed costs – especially in respect of floor space – are high all the time, not just at peak times. They can turn some fixed costs into variable costs, such as with temp staff. But they can't do that with all of their fixed costs.

Mastt has to live with high fixed costs all the time. Illiad wins because they can run almost on empty when the store is quiet.

It should be clear that it is not enough for Illiad to 'keep it small'. They have to – at the same time – 'speed it up.' For instance, say that shoppers shop at the same speed at both stores. Then Mastt should make up to twice as much as Illiad in sales, gross profit and OP. Illiad needs to 'speed it up' as well as 'keep it small', or it's like one hand trying to wash itself.

To keep it simple I first showed the gains from keeping it small, and then brought in the impact of speeding it up. It's hard to tell apart the gains from these two effects.

In the next few topics I look at how to speed things up in practice. There might be scores of ways that I failed to spot. The reader is bound to find other ways if they observe what is done in Small Two stores.

Topic 36: How to speed it up

I'VE SAID THAT a retail grocer can make more operating profit (OP) if they sell more goods in the same amount of time. One way to do this is to get shoppers to shop faster. It may be a good idea to ask shoppers (us) how this might be done. We could use some of the tried and tested ideas about flow rate to prompt us.

We should look at all the things in the store that could be done faster. So, where to start? We know from Topic 8 that the best place to start when we want to speed up flow rate is with the bottlenecks. Find them and get rid of them. One way to find bottlenecks is to look for where queues form. That leads to our first answer: in retail stores, queues form at the checkouts.

Other questions can follow on from that. How long do shoppers take to walk through the store? Or to walk to and from the parking area? How long do they take to find the brand they want? How quickly do the staff fill the shelves?

We should not expect to know the answers off pat. The answers lie in the real world, not in our heads. We should be forced to look at real data. It's no good if we start by asking 'could they serve twice as many shoppers in the same space?' This would try to force an answer before we have looked at the facts. We can't expect to know the answer as soon as we've read the question, as if this were an exam.

Instead we should ask, for each step in the process, 'what would it take to go faster?' Then we should observe what they do in actual stores. Only then can we think about it, and make a list of what we think it would take to go faster. If we can't do this right away we may want to rephrase our question. Or look for more facts. After one or two tries we can move on.

The point is that we have live models to observe – all the Small Two stores. We don't need their blessing to walk up and down their aisles. Also, as shoppers, we can judge for ourselves – we don't need to ask the official experts. If, when we start, we are unsure of the facts, we can make them up. Assume they are true. Later we can relax these assumptions one at a time. We start with 'twice the speed' as it's easy to work with; later we can change that.

It's not only the store that makes more money from a faster shopping flow. Shoppers have more time to spend on leisure. They, too, value their time.

There are three places where shopping speed is a factor. These are in the parking zone, at the till, and in the aisles. In this topic we look at the first of these three. How big should the parking zone be for an Illiad store? How does that compare with a Mastt store of the same size?

Let's say that in an Illiad store, twice as many cars exit the parking zone each hour. This makes room for twice as many to enter the zone. But each car stays there for half the time. Thus while more cars enter, more cars exit. The faster the shopping, the more cars will pass through. This shows that the size of the zone depends on the size of the store. That is, on its capacity, not its throughput. The store capacity depends on the size of the trading area. So the size of the parking zone depends on the size of the trading area. Not on the time taken to shop.

Each store group will have their own standards based on what goes on in their own stores. The exact parking ratio will vary for each one.

What about time saved by the shopper? The smaller the parking zone, the less time it takes to walk to and from the store. But if an Illiad store is half the size of a Mastt store it might not halve the walking time. If you draw two rectangles, one inside the other and half its area, it's clear that walking time might not halve, but it'll still be quicker.

In the next topic I look at the two main places where shopping speed is a factor: at the till and in the aisles.

Topic 37: Fast shopping: 1996

ILLIAD CASE STUDY (fiction). Excerpt of a meeting between Illy and Homer in March 1996.

HG: "Please tell me how you halve the checkout time?"

II: "Checkout time can be split into three. The first is how long a shopper waits in the queue. The second is how long the cashier takes to process a sale. And the third is how long the shopper takes to pack. The key is to think of these tasks as being done with many shoppers in parallel, not with one shopper at a time, in series.

"We like to open a new till point before the shopper gets restless from being in a queue. We don't want our shoppers to wait. It's a waste of their time. We use a rule of thumb to work out when to open a new till point.

"We tried out many rules of thumb. Most of these meant that the cashier would have to count. But that meant mental work when they were busy. They would have had to work it out each time. We didn't want that. We wanted them to just have to use their eyes.

"So we came up with the rule we use now. Say that a queue goes past the end of a counter; then the cashier at that till point must buzz for a staff member to open another one. All we had to do was make sure that counters are the right length. There must be room on a counter for the next person in a queue to load their goods. That's all. It has worked fine.

"The manager has to make sure that there are

enough staff to work all till points at peak times. Our stores have been designed to have enough till points at peak times."

HG: "I like it that they decide from the bottom up. No need for a manager or computer at a central point to decide from the top down. The cashier is at the right time and place."

II: "Only the rules are top down. Staff at the store use rules of thumb that we give them. We design most of our systems around the decisions that we want our staff to make. We want it to be people that make the judgement calls. Not computers. It helps our staff to keep their eyes open. It puts them on our side and in control of the results. It should be the person who is closest to the action at the time. We just have to give them rules of thumb that work."

HG: "You say that there should be room for a shopper to unload their trolley. If that is the case then at no time would a shopper have to stand in the queue with nothing to do. So that at no time would a shopper be idle. You keep your staff busy, but you also keep your shoppers busy."

II: "Sure. Wasted time costs money, no matter whose time it is. The shopper would have had to pay in some way. At the end of the day the money saved goes to the shopper. We only make more profit if we get more sales.

Checkout wizards

"The next thing that takes time is how long the cashier takes to process the sale. At a Mastt shop, the speed is whatever suits the shopper. Not so with us. Where

Mastt checks out maybe fifteen items per minute through the till, with our guys it's more than twice that [1].

"We have a smart way to dock the trolley at the till. The shopper can sweep some items into the trolley instead of doing it one at a time. We use giant bar codes on our store brands. A cashier can pass the items through the barcode reader faster than the shopper can pack them. All staff are trained to scan fast. Scan rates are part of team incentives. That means managers as well: they may have to work the tills at peak times.

"It makes sense for the shopper to pack their goods after they have been checked out. It's a separate process that doesn't need to be done at the checkout desk. It saves time for the cashier. They don't have to wait and do nothing while the shopper packs."

HG: "How long does it take the first-time shopper to get used to this?"

II: "It takes a few visits. Once they notice how much time they save, they get into the habit. I think people learn in the same way as they do when they learn to drive cars in traffic."

Speedy staff

HG: "Do your staff get used to always being in a hurry?"

II: "There's no time to get bored. They are cross-trained to do each other's work. This balances the load so that the brunt does not fall on just one person. Bear in mind that we hire staff who like to work that way. If it doesn't suit them it's better for them and us that they move on.

"Staff also spend less time with shoppers. Mastt

staff have to drop what they are doing to attend to shopper queries. Ours have to do the same so as not to give offence to shoppers. But it wastes time and drives costs up. So we have to look at it as if through the wrong end of a telescope. We start with the desired effect [2]. Then we ask: how do you gear up the store so that shoppers have few queries?

"The first step is for all staff to know the answers. They should not have to ask other staff or look it up. Stock is topped up all the time during the day, so if it's not on the shelves it should not be in the store. But sometimes it doesn't work that way: there is a gap in the shelves. If so, all staff know how and where to check, fast, if it's in the back. They know because they all stack shelves.

"Staff don't know what stock will be on sale in future promotions. So they're being honest when they say things like 'I don't know', and 'if it's not on the shelf it's not in the store.'

"Mastt likes to rearrange shelves to keep shoppers in the store for longer, but it wastes shoppers' time and causes more queries. We like to keep shoppers in the store for shorter."

Trim the range

HG: "Critics say that your product range is too small. Where does that fit in with shopping speed?"

II: "We know that with a small range of SKUs, shopping is fast. If they have 40k SKUs and we have 1k, then it's faster to shop with us. If they have five brands per product and we have one, then they have just 8k products. It means their range is only eight times as big as ours. Then a lot of their standard lines aren't groceries so they might have only twice our grocery range. We focus on groceries, and they don't. They have a much wider scope. So the gap is not as big as it looks.

"Where there is less choice there is less stress [3]. And it takes less time. Most of the time we let them choose from two types, standard or premium. We now think that with some products the shopper should have a choice of three items, not two: they choose faster and have less doubt about their choice [4]. They can go high, go low, or take the middle way. So, one of these days we may give shoppers a choice of three Illiad brands. The shopper would choose which one suits them. So I agree that you have a fair point. Our range may still be a bit too small."

HG: "When it comes to range the internet wins. So staying focused has clearly paid off for you. Yet I've seen quite a few lines in your stores that are not groceries."

II: "We stock a lot of non-grocery lines. But we stock those lines one at a time, not all at once. They are part of our impulse range: we change them every week.

"The impulse items might not be on the shopper's list. But that's the whole point. They buy them on impulse when they see them. If there were no impulse lines, there'd be no thrill of delight. All they'd get would be that warm glow as they look at their receipt and work out how much they've saved. The impulse lines also help to get them to come back each week. Apart from that, who wants a thrill when they shop for groceries?

"The thing about impulse lines is that people make their choices fast. They don't dawdle much."

HG: "How do you use your store format to cut down dawdling time?"

II: "We don't play music in the stores. First, it signals 'no frills'. Second, music may distract them; they start to daydream and take longer to shop. In our stores they are less likely to slip into a comfort zone; we don't let them forget the reason they are there. In brief, we like to keep their shopping experience simple. We don't base this on a deep theory. As you know, we do things based on if they work for us, not if we've been told that it's the thing to do. We do it if we find it takes shoppers less time to shop and our sales go up.

"We use big price tags that are easy for staff to change. We have bare skeleton shelves. We use wire netting so that our shelves are transparent. We often sell straight off the supplier's pallet. You might say that, behind all this, we do base it on some idea about why people do things. Our décor says to them, look, we don't waste money on bling, that's why we can sell things so cheaply. We're frugal so you can be frugal. That's what all this bare bones stuff is about."

HG: "So your approach is not only a signal to shoppers that they won't have to pay for frills. It also helps them to shop fast. What else is there?"

II: "As the British athletic teams say, it's to do with marginal gains. There's fifty years of small changes made by thousands of past and present staff. Most of it is on show in all the stores. Any shopper can see it. Rivals can see it and do the same if they want to. There are no secrets."

TOPIC 37 NOTES

[1] See also Thomas Rudolph, Bodo B Schlegelmilch, Josep Franch, Andras Bauer and Jan Niklas Meise (Eds.), 'Diversity in European Marketing: Text and Cases' (Wiesbaden: Springer Gabler, 2012), 144.
[2] Steve Jobs and Jeff Bezos both said 'Start with the customer and work backwards'". See google.co. uk/ #safe= active&q= start+ with+ the+ customer+ and+ work+ backwards and amazon. jobs/ principles; Russell Ackoff said: "Envision your ideal solution: then, work backwards to where you are": see Russel L Ackoff, 'Re-creating the Corporation' (New York: Oxford University Press, 1999).
[3] Gerd Gigerenzer, 'Gut Feelings' (USA: Viking Penguin, 2007), 33. He writes that shoppers say that they prefer a wide choice, yet they buy more if they are faced with less choice. However, I can't find hard evidence to show that this applies where there are just a few items to choose from.
[4] This assertion sounds plausible but I can't recall reading any evidence which supports or refutes it. The reader may want to check in Daniel Kahneman: 'Thinking Fast and Slow' (UK: Penguin, 2012); or Herbert A Simon on satisficing: en.wikipedia. org/ wiki/ Satisficing.

Topic 38: Arithmetic: 1996

Illiad Case Study (fiction). Excerpt of a meeting between Illy and Homer in June 1996.

II: "I want to know if you know how flow rate works, but I don't want the theory. Tell me what would be the effect on profit if shoppers were to take half the time to shop. Give me a 'for instance'."

HG: "Fine. I'll assume a few things to start with.

"Say you have one store. The store is always filled with shoppers. A shopper takes one hour to shop from start to finish. From when they enter the store until when they leave it. Say that one new shopper enters each minute. If we start at opening time, after an hour there will be sixty shoppers in the shop. From then on, each time one leaves, a new one enters. So there will be sixty shoppers in the shop at all times. Except for the first and last hours of the day."

II: "Fine. I can see that if one comes in each minute, in an hour there will be sixty of them. No-one leaves in the first hour because they need that hour to shop. From then on, each minute a shopper pays and leaves, and a new one comes in. So with one in and one out there will always be sixty in the shop. Except for the first and last hours."

HG: "Okay. So now we can do the arithmetic, step by step. And I'll work with averages. Ignore the first and last hours.

"We know that the 'number of shoppers in the shop' is 60. And we know that the 'time it takes for one shopper to shop' is 1 hour.

"We want to know the 'number of shoppers who do their shopping per hour'. That is the same as 'how many shoppers flow through the shop each hour.'

"We divide 60 by 1, which gives 60. That's the shopper flow rate per hour. Or, throughput. Okay?"

II: "Sure, if you divide 60 by 1 you get 60. We must divide how many there are in the shop by the time it takes for one of them to shop. The flow rate here is 60 shoppers per hour. But what if more than one of them arrives each minute, ready to shop?"

HG: "The capacity of the store is 60 people. At peak times there are more than 60 people who would like to shop there. If the extra people don't want to wait they go elsewhere. And it's peak time at least once a day."

II: "That would bring tears to my eyes! Who would throw away money like that? I'd want to know who's to blame."

HG: "Fine. You own the store. So you might want to take the blame ... but don't worry, this is not for real. Now, Mastt and Illiad each solve the problem in their own way. Mastt buys and builds on the ground next door, so they now have twice the space. They also have twice the parking space. They buy twice as many cash tills and other odds and ends. This means that 120 shoppers now fit into their store.

"We want to know how many shoppers can flow through the shop each hour. We take 120 and divide by 1 to get 120. This means that 120 shoppers can flow through the shop each hour. That's the 'flow rate' (or 'throughput'). If the store is full at peak times then its sales per hour at peak times are twice as much as before. So their gross profit is up to twice as much as Illiad at peak times. Their running costs (fixed costs) are less than twice as much because they won't need, say, more than one manager. We can't know their exact operating profit (OP) because we don't know how many hours are peak times. Note that peak times are not all the time; but fixed costs are all the time."

II: "Why didn't you just say that with a store of twice the size you can make up to twice the OP?"

HG: "I had to spell it out so you can see that I know how it works. Let me go on ... at Illiad's, as I said, they do it in their own way. They can't buy the shop next door, so they can't make their shop bigger. Instead, they sort things out so that their shoppers take half the time to shop. They take half an hour instead of one hour."

II: "Okay. So if they shop more quickly, then the store sales go up. But please talk me through that."

HG: "Half an hour is 0.5 of an hour. Now divide 60 by 0.5 and you get 120. That gives you the flow rate (or throughput) per hour.

"To show how that works: we can still fit only 60 shoppers in the store. One new shopper enters the store each half-minute. The first 60 will have come into the store by the end of the first half-hour. After that, each half-minute, one leaves the store and one comes in. That means that the number in the store stays the same at 60.

"Yet if 60 shoppers leave each half hour, it means that 120 leave each hour. So 120 of them will have shopped each hour. That's the same as the big Mastt store."

It's not just speed

II: "Right: it seems that you've got it. But what about the cash tills? Would you have to squeeze in twice as many?"

HG: "There are two cases to look at. The first is, let's say, we have to squeeze in twice as many cash tills and other stuff. In this case, Illiad makes the same sales as a Mastt store; yet it makes quite a bit more OP because it saves on rent. And rent can be as high as 5pc of sales." (See Topic 34).

II: "Okay. That on its own could more than double their OP. What's the second case?"

HG: "Now let's say that none of your fixed costs go up. Your checkout throughput is twice as fast, so you don't need more tills. Your staff may unload deliveries faster – there's no need to move twice as fast: they may unload more on each trip. Or they unload twice as often: they walk half as far because the store is half the size. The main thing is that your OP will exceed theirs by how much you save in extra fixed costs.

"Worst case is you just save on rent. Best case is you save on all fixed costs. Both shops do the same sales; you just make more OP. Note that at this stage we can still assume that the quality of the products of both firms is the same."

II: "Okay, so we make more OP on each pound of sales. What's your point?"

HG: "Two points. First, you could pass on that extra OP to your shoppers with lower prices. You could tweak it so that your OP per hour would be the same as Mastt. You could do this, even though your gross margin – gross profit as a per cent of sales – would now be less than theirs."

II: "Why would I want to pass on the extra OP to my shoppers?"

HG: "Because they will notice. If they get the same quality at a lower price, more of them will come back."

II: "What if they don't find it convenient? Or if they think they're being pushed?"

HG: "Don't push them to shop too fast. That way, you cut your fixed costs but not by so much as to inconvenience them. By now you will have learnt how much you can tweak this to get the best results. And you know that when you get right down to it, with groceries, shoppers like to be able to do it fast."

II: "Okay. You said 'first.' What's your second point?"

HG: "There is a myth that costs can be pushed down in only two ways. One part of the myth is that Mastt can pay less for their stock because of their 'huge buying power'. This lets them 'squeeze their suppliers' more than you can. The other part of the myth is that to pay less for your stock you need to 'skimp on quality.' People don't see how one firm can do the same things at less cost than another firm. They may find the concept of efficiency – to do more with less – hard to grasp. In this case, it costs you less because you take less time and space to get the same throughput."

II: "Okay, Homer, that's fine. I had to know that you grasp the details.

"Speaking of formulas, I know that this one is as easy as 'A is B times C' [1]. But, just remind me, what does A stand for again?"

HG: "'A' stands for how many shoppers in the shop at a time, which is like your 'stock' of shoppers. 'B' stands for the time that a shopper takes to shop. 'C' stands for how many shoppers do their shopping in a time period: that is, the flow rate or throughput of your 'stock'."

II: "Yes, but I see that you had to divide two of them to get the third one?"

HG: "I cross-multiplied. We want to find out how much C is. If A equals B times C then C equals A divided by B. You may recall that to get there you divide both sides by the same thing, in this case B."

II: "Of course I knew that!"

HG: "Yet some people say: but this is so simple it's trivial. It's all obvious. Then you ask them why don't they all do it? Don't they know that shoppers would prefer to pay less?"

II: "You mean, shoppers think why-pay-more? I can tell you that only some of them think that way. Especially in a rich country like the UK."

HG: "As long as at least twenty per cent of them think why-pay-more then you'll be fine. Who knows, it may turn out to be more than twenty per cent."

TOPIC 38 NOTES

[1] See coursera. org/ learn/ wharton-operations/ lecture/ kyo5e/ littles-law and en.wikipedia. org/ wiki/ Little's_law.

Topic 39: Finding flow: 2015

ILLIAD CASE STUDY (fiction). Excerpt of a meeting between Illy and Homer in May 2015.

II: "Flow rate and Little's Law have been used in sectors like fast food [1]. But none of the Mastt grocers seem to have used it in the way that you and I have spoken about. If they have, why have we not seen signs of it in the market? Or in the media?"

HG: "Well, as you know, flow rate plays a big part when you manage stock in the supply chain [2]. It has to do with stock throughput. The more often you can turn over – buy and sell – your stock, then the less your cost of holding it. That's the same as saying that the faster the flow rate the lower the holding cost, and the higher the return on investment in stock. Little's Law covers all of that.

"The way we use it here is to talk of shoppers as if they were items of stock. We aim to speed up the flow of that stock item (shoppers) through the store."

II: "I don't quite get that?"

HG: "We can speed up the flow rate of shoppers in one of two ways. We can boost the number of shoppers in the shop at one time. That's like the old mantra: 'pile 'em high'. Or we can boost the speed at which they move through the shop. That's more like part of the new mantra: 'speed it up.' The faster we can get shoppers to flow through the store, the more shoppers will get to shop each day."

II: "Of course. It means we can do more sales and gross profit each day."

HG: "Note that it's no big deal, just a simple idea. What is quite hard to do is to work out how to make it happen. You've done it well because you worked on it over many years, a bit at a time."

II: "Yes. Small stores have helped us to speed up the shoppers' search for the product they want. Having only a few brands has helped us to speed up the shoppers' choice of brand. For them it's first fast search; then it's fast choice. We restock our shelves so fast and often that our trading space is more like a showroom. All that shoppers want is a place for them to look, choose, pay, pack and move on. It means that shoppers spend less time in the store. It makes more room for others to shop.

"But when they worked out this whole supply chain process, why did they not extend it a bit? Why didn't they apply it to shoppers, and treat them like stock?"

HG: "I suppose that people and stock were not seen as quite the same thing. Stock played such a big part in retail at the time; to cut down the cost of holding it was first on their list. For them to then apply it to people they would have had to put low prices and shopping speed first.

"At that time, the big idea was to meet the needs of all their shoppers. Firms had loyalty cards to keep track of what their shoppers bought. They used IT to match what was bought with what they could stock. They could then tailor their offers to shoppers, on a one-to-one basis. But they still looked at it from the point of view of the retailer and their products.

"They also may have had a balance sheet point of

view, like in a manufacturing firm. They would want to push up their percentage 'return on assets'. One way to do that is to boost the return (profit) on the assets (stock); the other way to do that is to have the same return but to reduce the assets. That's what they did.

"But a services firm has a profit and loss account point of view. They want to push up their 'return (profit) on sales'. As you and I have discussed, these are the gross and operating margins. To do that, they try to push up sales and reduce costs. Assets are not the thing. Not in a services firm."

II: "Sixty years ago we tried to find out what the grocery shopper wants. We found out quite soon that they want fast and cheap shopping. Since then we've tried our best to give them that. No need to make it more complex. The internet has made 'fast and cheap' trendy, but we've been doing it for a few decades."

HG: "There was a time when one-to-one shopping was brand new. It took years for all the big groups to get in on it. By then, shoppers were not so sure that all these stores really wanted to look after them. But you guys went your own way early on."

II: "We found our point of focus. Now we change as slowly as we can. We change things one at a time, and then we observe results. If it works we roll it out with many stores, then we check again.

"We drive all the changes ourselves. We may use consultants to help carry things through. But on the strategy side we dare not outsource. We do that on our own. We talk with people like you to help us stay on track.

"Our main thing is to look after the shopper."

HG: "That sounds fine. Shoppers like it just as much as you do. We know that the Mastt store groups are not yet into it. So you might have a clear run, and get to the number of stores that you want without a hitch.

The end is nigh

"But I think Little's Law as it applies to shoppers will hit the big time soon. There are at least two reasons. One is online shopping. The other is firms like yours. Had there been no online shopping, Mastt might have had to shift up a little while you took a bigger market share. You might have reached 30pc but not much more.

"Now, with the internet, it's all changed. Online shops don't need to rent trading space. You come along and show that a bricks-and-mortar store can halve its trading space. Online has the edge, but you've chipped away at their edge because you found that you can swap time for space. How can Mastt compete with that?

"You may say: why do they have to compete with that? The answer is that their running costs are too high. Shoppers prefer to pay less for the same thing.

"In a few years a third of all retail sales may be online (see Topic 57). By then there may have been a big shakeout in the world of retail. There could be mayhem by 2020. Grocers will be better off than the rest of retail but they can't escape. They still have to compete with the grocer next door. So by then Mastt will have had to have learnt to swap time for space. Click and collect won't be enough; on the ground, they still have to compete with the likes of your group."

II: "But surely all the big consulting firms know

about Little's Law?"

HG: "I'm sure they all do. It would be just one of a vast array in their bag of tricks. They might not name it as such: they can't claim to own Little's formula as a piece of IP. It's in the public domain. But it can be part of their bag of tricks.

"Shopping speed may be the next big thing. The trigger that makes it happen would be a combo of online shopping, Little's Law and store groups like yours that know how to use flow rate.

"If so, the consulting firms will be able to bring it on stream with their clients straight away. It might not be as big as reengineering was in the nineties [3], but it could still be big. Its beauty as a bandwagon is that it's so quick to learn that anyone can jump on board. Yet it has a lot of power so it needs to be handled with care."

TOPIC 39 NOTES

[1] See also: people.cs.umass. edu/ ~emery/ classes/ cmpsci691st/ readings/ OS/ Littles-Law-50-Years-Later. pdf
[2] Gerard Cachon and Christian Terwiesch, 'Matching Supply with Demand: An Introduction to Operations Management' (New York: McGraw-Hill Irwin, 2006).
[3] Michael Hammer and James Champy, 'Reengineering the Corporation: A Manifesto for Business Revolution' (London: Nicholas Brealey Publishing, 1993).

Topic 40: Missing flow: 1996

Illiad Case Study (fiction). Excerpt of a meeting between Illy and Homer in May 1996.

II: "How come none of our rivals have clicked that to cut down shopping time is as good as adding space? And that they could make more profit by doing so?"

HG: "I think I know why. Say that a shop is half full most of the time. Now say that, all at once, shoppers shop twice as fast. The only real change is that the shop will be a quarter full most of the time. It won't change the operating profit (OP).

"The same applies if, to start with, the shop is full most of the time. If shoppers were to shop at twice the speed then the shop would be half full most of the time. Once again, it won't change the OP.

"It all changes when too many people want to shop, that is, at peak times. If shoppers shop at twice the speed, it's as if the store has twice the floor space. So if the store would be more than full at peak times then you can make more gross profit in those peak times. But peak times are not the same at all stores. At one shop, it may be only on a single day in December. At others, it may be on a few days a year. Yet others may have peak times a few times a month, or at certain times daily.

"That's when fast shopping starts to count. But you can't put out a notice to shoppers to say please shop fast at rush hour. You can't train them to shop fast for some of the time; it has to be all the time or not at all.

You can't be pushy. In fact, you have to nudge them all the way [1]. That starts with how you design the store, the displays, the payment area, the parking, the lot. All the things to do with running the store. It all has to have been designed that way, long before, as part of how you wanted to run the firm.

"At the first sign of congestion Mastt might have thought it best to add more space. Rather than to rejig the logistics in the store to speed things up. Why try to solve a problem that may take place only once a year?"

II: "They might not have noticed that the cost of more space – like rent – has to be borne all the time, not just at peak times."

HG: "That's right: it might not have crossed their mind to make time instead of space. But even had they thought of it, they might not have done it. Why not? Stores looked for ways to coax shoppers to stay in the store for longer. They didn't want shoppers to hurry. Why not? Because they wanted to sell them the non-basic lines. Shoppers need to browse for those lines.

"When stores boosted their range, it would have slowed shopping down. One risk of their trying to hurry up shoppers is that they might have got rid of those who like to browse. Also, the ones who like to shop out of town may be the same ones who like to browse. Product range and shopper type may be linked. The link may be so tight that if you break up the one you lose the other. Maybe that's why they didn't want to tinker with shopping speed."

II: "But it's more likely they just failed to notice the impact of flow rate. So it's back to my first question. How come they didn't see it in the first place?"

HG: "Here's why it's hard to see at first. Say that you visit Stores A and B on Monday. You count fifty shoppers in each. You do your count every hour. It's always fifty. In both shops. At the end of the day you are told that both shops opened and closed at the same time; that the average number of shoppers in both stores was fifty throughout the day; and that the average spent by each shopper was the same. Yet at closing time on Monday you are told that B's sales were twice those of A. How come?"

[Ed: If you ask someone who has not read this book, would they get it?]

"By now it may be clear. The shoppers in B shop at twice the speed of those in A; there was time for twice as many shoppers to shop at B, so B got twice the sales. Now, why might you not have noticed this fact?

"Each time you looked in on the shops, you could take in the 'space' in a glance. Each glance gave you a picture at a point in time. You could count the number of shoppers in one go. It was always fifty. But to take in the passage of time it would not help for you to count the number of shoppers at one time. Even if you counted a few times in one day. Even if you gave each one that you counted a red hat to wear so as not to count them twice.

"Knowing how many are in the store at one time tells you about capacity. That's no help. You want to know how many shopped that day. That tells you the flow rate, or throughput. The key is how fast they shop. To get that, you don't need to check every now and then. All you need to know at the end of the day is how many shoppers went through the checkout. You just need a count of the number of till slips.

"The answer to the last part of your question is also not obvious. You asked why, if you speed up shopping, you make more in extra profit than if you were just to add space? Well, if you add floor space you increase fixed costs – rent and so on. But it might cost you nothing more to speed up shopping."

TOPIC 40 NOTES

[1] Cass R Sunstein and Richard H Thaler, 'Nudge: Improving Decisions about Health, Wealth and Happiness' (USA: Penguin Books, 2009).

Topic 41: The story so far

THIS IS TO sum up the dilemma faced by Mastt in respect of fixed costs, such as rent and wages. It does not bring in the effect of store brands.

Mastt can't match Illiad's prices. One reason is that Mastt's fixed costs are higher.

There are two sides to Mastt's problem. If they try to match prices right now, they may lose money until they have none left. If they try to match prices in the longer term they'd have to lower their fixed cost structure. But to do that they'd need to change the way they do business. Most of their fixed costs come from high rent and wages. High rent comes from having large stores to cope with the wide product range. High wages come from having enough staff to run the large stores. How do they reduce rent in large stores? How do they reduce staff with no damage to service levels or staff morale?

That brings us to the other side of their problem. If they change the way they do business they may lose all their shoppers.

Case study (fiction): Illy and Homer spoke about this at a meeting in March 2015.

II: "Homer, you've told me things our rivals could start doing now if they wanted. Tell me about things we do now that they can't match?"

HG: "Your secret – and I don't know how many years you've got before they catch on – is flow rate. Your flow rate is fast for reasons they can't match. The small store size, quick checkout, narrow aisles, focused product range and lack of dead space. They can't begin to match your prices as long as they go on doing things the way they do."

II: "What's to stop them from trying?"

HG: "They'd have to start from scratch. They'd need to change from A to Z. If they do it too fast they may lose their shoppers. But if they don't change, they may still lose their shoppers, because of your lower prices. And if they try to match your prices before they change from A to Z, they may run out of cash."

CHAPTER 7: ISSUES

Topic 42: Growing: 1995

ILLIAD CASE STUDY (fiction). Excerpt of a meeting between Illy and Homer in June 1995.

HG: "You want to open more stores as fast as you can. But you want to do that out of past profits? Will you beef it up with money from the European side of your firm? Will you use debt?"

II: "Profits made in the UK stay in the UK. We use our UK profits to grow in the UK. Our shareholders don't need the dividends; we all have cash in the bank and don't need more for now. We don't use much debt.

"We've done it this way for a long time. Why grow faster? What's the rush? We're doing fine as we are."

HG: "I accept that it's a good idea to grow only at the rate of your profits. In good times you make more money and open more stores. In bad times you make less money but open fewer stores. So you grow more or less at the same pace as demand. But you must take a heck of a long-term view!"

II: "I don't work in order to retire one day. With me it's not just that I do it for a living – being a grocer is what I am. The family should live on long after I'm gone. They might run the firm in the same way. Or not."

HG: "Fine. But don't you think that you might lose out on some big growth? In a slowdown, when some guys might go bust, isn't that the right time to jump in?"

II: "No. The way we look at it is that 'when the market grows, we grow; when the market shrinks, we grow' [1].

"Jokes aside, it's hard to be the low-cost grocer in all markets. Once we have our 20pc market share in the UK, we'll see if we should go for more. There might be more why-pay-more shoppers than we thought."

TOPIC 42 NOTES

[1] CEO and founder Michael Dell interview with Bloomberg TV, 3rd Dec 2014: marketoracle.co. uk/ Article48497

Topic 43: Team building: 1996

I<small>LLIAD</small> C<small>ASE</small> S<small>TUDY</small> (fiction). Excerpt of a meeting between Illy and Homer in June 1996.

HG: "You said once that you like to deal with the same kind of people, whether they are staff or suppliers. Can you tell me what you mean?"

II: "We don't want free riders or bullies. We see both of these types as shirkers. Both are bad for business and try to get someone else to do their work. Most of the time we screen them out before they can sneak on board."

HG: "How do you do that?"

II: "Tough but clear standards seem to work the best. For instance, we require fifty hours of work per week for some jobs. We are open that it needs hard work. People know this when they apply. It attracts the kind of people we want. Shirkers tend to spot that the job is not for them. Once they realise there's no place to hide, they back off. And the sooner we find out the less it costs us.

"We pay staff more than our rivals do. So we tend to be top of the list of those who want a job in a supermarket. Just as shoppers like to pay less, staff like to be paid more. Both ways, we get first bite."

HG: "You don't seem to like shirkers?"

II: "Most people are fine to deal with. But there are free riders and bullies here and there. We think that they only act like that if the culture at their place of work lets them do it. We are lucky that in our line of work we can set clear targets. Our store teams are tight and small: up to around thirty people. It's hard for any-one in the team to hide what they're doing – or not do-ing – from the rest. But it's an ongoing story, so we can't drop our guard."

HG: "So clear standards can get rid of shirkers?"

II: "That, plus peer pressure to make sure they can't get away with it. Teams don't do well if one mem-ber throws or fails to pull their weight. The pay packet of the whole team is smaller. So shirkers get short shrift from the rest. We don't need spies or things like that to spot them: they are outed by their peers. The challenge for us is to match our reward systems with what people achieve."

HG: "What are the ideal traits of store staff?"

II: "We like them to be reliable and curious. And they need to work well in teams. Not much of what goes on in a store is complex. But it's vital for all staff to stay alert, and react fast to things that go on around them. Most of them love it – their jobs are all action. Those ones tend to stay."

HG: "So morale must be high?"

II: "Yes. That's the manager's main job. The hi-erarchy is flat, with only a few layers. Each team mem-ber knows what they have to do. The key is that they can swap jobs when they have to. And they want to do it because they have a team goal. They can think ahead about what needs to be done."

HG: "Is that why your staff turnover rate is low?"

II: "We think so. Teams tend to bind when they do a good job. And people like to be recognised and paid well [1]. Our job in running the firm is to create the climate for these things to happen.

"We think that people act in what they see as their own interests, and they respond to incentives. These must work for them as well as the firm. We measure results to compare them with other stores."

HG: "Your systems tell you all that?"

II: "Yes, we track items through the checkout in many ways. By the minute, by the cashier, by the time of day, and so on. We like to set things up so that people win most of the time. They get lots of feedback as to how well they are doing. With only a few standard store sizes we can compare like for like."

HG: "But don't things go wrong?"

II: "All the time. That's the same for all grocers, all firms and all people. We just try to start with the right structure and then do things one step at a time. Teamwork is built from working together. With staff, it's to be in a well-run store. With suppliers it's to take part in a series of good deals where both sides gain.

"To keep staff grounded we look to how local firms work. Look at village (town) markets. Why are they still in business? It's because they know what they're doing; they don't need bells and whistles to make it look good. One eye is always on the customer. We try to train our staff to think like market traders."

TOPIC 43 NOTES

[1] See also Marcus Buckingham and Curt Coffman, 'First Break All the Rules' (UK: Simon & Schuster, 1999).

Topic 44: Store brands: 1996

Illiad Case Study (fiction). Excerpt of a meeting between Illy and Homer in March 1996.

HG: "Can you tell me about your store brands?"

II: "We have two types of supplier that make our store brands. There are some firms where all they do is make store brands for firms like ours. Then there are those that make store brands as well as their own brands, which may be national brands.

"The specs of our store brand belong to us. The supplier has the sole right to supply us for the term of their contract."

HG: "Say that a large supplier makes your store brand for you. Do you still stock their national brand of that same type of product?"

II: "We stock almost no national brands. Here and there we may stock a household name. So this is not an issue for us. Mastt does face this sort of issue: they stock both the store brand and the national brand of a product."

HG: "So a supplier may prefer to make a store brand for you than for Mastt? The store brand they make for you would have no rivals. But the store brand they make for Mastt would have rival national brands on the shelves."

II: "That's true, but Mastt has more stores in the UK. So suppliers can get more sales in total if they supply all of the Mastt stores. What do you think is first prize for the big suppliers?"

HG: "It would be to supply their national brand

to Mastt. They would still own all the IP rights, so they can feel more secure. And they would still hold the reins. On the other hand, their rivals may be able to bid for the best spot on the shelves.

"Do you judge where to place stock on the shelves by sales value?"

II: "Not quite. We judge how well a line is doing based more or less on gross profit per square metre. But we place stock on the shelves where shoppers expect to see it. We try not to chop and change too much. The shopper can move fast because they know where the goods are.

"We set a gross margin for each category. That means that when the supplier drops their price we drop ours too. The shopper gains, straight off. We don't try to make the most profit that we can get away with for each product. That would go against the whole idea of EDLP. Only a few firms look at it the way we do – it's too easy to take one's eye off the ball.

"As I've said, to score a goal you glance at the posts to take aim. But you keep your eye on the ball (not the posts) as you kick it. The goal follows. In our case we keep our eye on giving the shopper the best deal. The profit follows."

HG: "Er ... sure. But why did Mastt let the FMCG firms decide where to place stock on shelves? Why did they hand over such a key role?"

II: "It may be a relic from the past. Big FMCG firms used to provide the cash for small firms to start up in retail. Some retail firms grew to be big in their own right. Later on, category management (CM) failed to live up to its claims. It should have moved the power from the big FMCG firms to the retail stores. But the FMCG firms were smart. They might have said, look, we're fine with CM, but we'll give you money for the best spots on the shelves, or the end-of-aisle displays. The retail stores said yes, and that's the way it's worked since then [1]. It's how the FMCG have kept their stock in good spots on the shelves for all these years. And, by the way, it's the same for all retail. The firms that make the goods want the retailer to give them a special spot on the shelves. If it's not allowed they might still do it, and call it something else."

HG: "Just remind me. What's the problem with that? If they're all happy? Too bad about the small suppliers who don't have the cash to do the same and fight back ... but so what?"

II: "Mastt forgets two key things. One: what do their shoppers want? The way shoppers give feedback is by what they buy. If they are nudged into buying what they don't quite want they'll still buy it. For now. Until firms like us come along. Mastt might not know if a product was bought because of the special discount or because of the product. We need to know what products the shopper really wants. Feedback from them is like gold to us. But we don't have to use focus groups or surveys. We just watch what they buy. Then we can give it to them – at our best price.

"It does not help us if a shopper buys a product because they think it's a bargain. All that tells us is that that shopper likes a bargain. What helps us is when they buy the product that they like at the stated price. That is what we'd like to know. It's about the product and its price. Not about a shopper's state of mind.

"Then Mastt forgets a second key thing. They think they can grant to the shopper the power of choice. But that's not true. The shopper just takes the power. Once they have the choice. When firms are free to compete, the shopper has the choice. We try to have a level playing field for all our lines. So the shopper is free to choose what they like. That's why we don't have displays at the end of each aisle. If we did, we wouldn't know if the shopper had gone for the product or for its prime spot on the shelves."

HG: "What's to stop Mastt doing the same?"

II: "They have too much at stake in what they've got. Thousands of hours are used up on working out deals. It's a vast network of people and rules. Make no mistake: they have smart people and smart rules. But they are bound up by their ways, their firm's culture. It's bound up in their standards: the rules by which they decide things; in their procedures, that are guided by these rules; and in their people, whose skills are honed by what they do each day. Yet they might change. Who knows?

"One day most stores are going to have to do the same things we do. That is, give the shopper what they want for as cheap as they can, and with no frills or fancy talk. Then we'll have to join the worry queue. But until then we are free to do things the way we like it."

Store brand slam dunk

HG: "Okay, I get that. But why else are store brands so good for the retailer? And what's your risk if you don't stock national brands?"

II: "We own the IP rights to our store brands.

When a supplier enhances a product, we just add that to our specs. If things go wrong we can switch suppliers fast. If the new ones can't match the cost price right away, they can at least match the specs right away. Suppliers can't hold us to ransom like they can with national brands [2]. We place a high value on our IP.

"It's true that we own lots of stores in Europe. That makes suppliers want to deal with us: they might get the export sales. But the buying power that goes with size has less effect on gross margins than some claim.

"For instance, let me ask you about real savings. How come we can sell our store brands for so much less than national brands of the same standard?"

HG: "The supplier of a national brand has to spend money to promote it. That cost is passed on to the store. But that same supplier would not need to spend money to promote your store brand. That cuts your cost of sales in one go by about a third [3]. That is a huge saving. It dwarfs what Mastt might save on national brands based on their buying power.

"Shoppers trust the quality of national brands. That's why they pay more for them. But your store brands have been around for so long that they look like national brands: your shoppers have learnt to trust them as if they were. Yet your store brands still cost you a third less. They have great pulling power in their own right. That's why you can afford to place a high value on your IP. It's worth it."

II: "Have you worked out how much we stand to gain from our store brands?"

HG: "Here's a rough guess. Let's say that all your

brands were store brands and that Mastt had no store brands. If their cost of sales was (round figures) 75pc of sales then yours would be one third less, or around 50pc of sales. You could drop your prices by a third and still make the same gross margins that they do.

"But it's more likely that half of their brands are now store brands. That means you could cut your selling prices by a sixth – half of a third – and still make the same gross margins that they do. But as I don't know the sales mix, this is quite a crude thumb suck.

"We know that your fixed costs are 8pc less than theirs. Add to that the one sixth (17pc) you save in your store brand margins, and your costs are one quarter (25pc) less than theirs. You could cut your prices by a quarter and still make the same 5pc operating margin that they make."

II: "That guess is close enough. We'll use it for now."

Easy as pies

HG: "Okay. So, how do you choose a supplier to make one of your store brands?"

II: "I'll tell you, but this is not for real. It's just to show the principle behind it. Say we want to bring in a soup range. We first find out what Mastt stores do. Let's say that their selling price is £2 and their cost price is £1.20. That gives them a gross profit of eighty pence; and a gross margin of 40pc.

"We first decide how much cheaper we want to go. Let's say the sweet spot for our shoppers is to pay 25pc less for the soup than they would pay Mastt. So we would sell the soup for £1.50. Our cost price would be

£1.20, the same as Mastt. That gives us a gross profit of thirty pence; that is, a gross margin of 20pc (versus 40pc).

"We give all our suppliers a rough recipe to work on, and then we ask them to pitch. Finally we choose our supplier and do the deal."

HG: "So the shopper pays 50 pence (25pc) less for the soup, and your gross profit of 30 pence is less than half that of Mastt's 80 pence."

II: "Well, we don't see it as half; we see it as a margin of 20pc less than theirs. We like to have a margin of 10pc to 40pc points less than our rivals.

"In this case we might also go for a premium soup. We'd pay the supplier say £1.36 pence (not £1.20) and sell it for £1.70 (not £1.50) to get a gross profit of 34 pence; and the same gross margin of 20pc. That extra 16 pence means our suppliers can spend quite a bit more on herbs and spices."

HG: "So you both agree on the exact recipe in each case?"

II: "That's right. It's our recipe, and our IP. We know what their gross profit is. We want them to do a good job. When the contract expires we might renew it with them, or not. It depends on how good a job they've done and how close we are to our sales targets."

HG: "Why don't all big supermarkets just sell store brands? I mean, they all know how much cheaper they are? And being so big they can create a national image for each of their own brands?"

II: "Well, we can assume they all know that store brands are a third cheaper [4]. But they have done fine as they are, so far. So why change? You tell me."

HG: "Sixty years ago in the UK all the big family grocery chains had their own store brands. The discounters at that time brought in national brands; they worked hand-in-glove with the big FMCG firms to get big volumes and low margins. The pendulum is just swinging back again."

TOPIC 44 NOTES

[1] See also thisismoney.co. uk/ money/ markets/ article-2780604/ hidden-fees-fuel-supermarket-profits - Suppliers-charged-80-000-just-new-products- store-shelves
[2] See also: thesun.co. uk/ living/ 1975899/ marmite - brexit-battle-shows-how-unilever-and-other-retail-giants-control-most-of-the-food-we-buy
[3] See plma. com/ storeBrands/ facts2015 and forbes. com/ 2011/ 06/ 29/ 10-secrets-about-store-brands
[4] See plma. com/ halloffame3

Topic 45: Suppliers: 1996

ILLIAD CASE STUDY (fiction). Excerpt of a meeting between Illy and Homer in May 1996.

II: "Most of our stock consists of store brands. We use a wide range of suppliers. They may be small and local firms or, at the top end, they may be multinationals. What do you think we gain from having mainly store brands – apart from less cost?"

HG: "You call the shots. They can't mess you around. There's only one route for them to go. They have to give you the quality you agreed on."

II: "Mastt could do the same as us, couldn't they? They could stock just their own store brands. Right?"

HG: "No. The secret of Mastt's past success is that they give the shopper a huge range to choose from. It would be risky for them to get rid of all their national brands. They need to stock a full range, so that the shopper feels they have a wide choice. That's one main reason shoppers go to Mastt. If they can't get the wide choice they might switch stores.

"But let me ask you about your store brands. What makes you choose to sell it as a premium product? And is there a halo effect [1], so that if they like the product it makes them like Illiad too?"

II: "At present, we may have both a standard and a premium version. We use price to signal that they differ. Thus our price for our two brands of coffee might be £1.50 and £2 per bag. The main thing is that we make it clear that they have a choice. Then there does seem to be a halo effect.

"With bigger stores we'd bring in a third choice."

HG: "Why do your shoppers like your store brands? Despite the fact you have so few national brands for them to compare with?"

II: "It's been a long road to get into the market. We built up our store brands from scratch. We got the shopper in the door with low prices. We made sure the quality was good enough for them to come back.

"Then we did one more thing that has paid off big time. Each category comprises a range of products. That entire range is sold under its own brand name. That brand name is in fact one of our store brands. At first we did this so that the shopper would remember the name. Then we found that they latched onto these store brand names. Many of them think of them as national brands that are exclusive to us. We think that this has worked better than if we'd just had one name for our full range of store brands, such as Illiad's Best."

Negotiate to win-win

HG: "May I ask how you get your buyers and supplier to work to the same aim?"

II: "Tough love. Each year we cull up to twenty per cent of our lines. That's based on how much gross profit they make. We replace the duds with new lines. If it's a store brand we change its recipe. No supplier wants their product to be one of the duds. So it forces their rep and our buyer to work as a team. They do so as joint problem-solvers. They come up with things like smart design and packaging. It may be cheaper, or it may improve the look, or it may take less shelf space."

HG: "Rivals of yours have said that some of your

store brands are a rip-off of national brands. Does that make you cross?"

II: "They can't say that we rip off their brand, because their specs are a secret. It may be that the logo or image of one of our store brands looks like a copy of one of theirs. Then they should be flattered. We would not cross the line and risk being sued. But if a recipe is well-known we'll use it; our rivals have no right to stop us [2]. We won't leave an open goal for them to sell food at monopoly prices."

HG: "You said that you like to deal with the right people to start with. What's the right kind of supplier?"

II: "We think there are two main ways to negotiate in our kind of business. One is to solve problems. The other is to be adversarial. The first way gets good results most of the time. The second way gets poor results most of the time [3]. We train our own buyers to use the first way. Suppliers pick that up from the way our buyers deal with them. They soon learn to do the same.

"One of our mottos is 'best price first.' From the outset we do it that way and tell them we expect them to do it. It helps make deals happen fast and puts things on an even keel from the start. It blows away the ones who try to get too smart."

HG: "Do you own some of your suppliers? In order to control your chain of supply from its source?"

II: "We don't do that at all. A snag with one link is a snag for the whole chain. Now, if one link goes, we find a new one to replace it. Our supply chain is strong because it's a chain of linked modules. It's not an unbroken rod that may snap under pressure. We don't have to carry the losses of our supplier as well as our own. We just do what we're good at – which is to sell groceries. But there are two sides to this. I don't say that our way is the one true way. I'm just saying this is what we do."

HG: "Fine. I would think you'd need far fewer staff to do your buying than Mastt. You stock fewer than twelve hundred lines to their tens of thousands. This must mean a lot less work?"

II: "Yes. Of course, much of our buying is done by the regions: it's not all done from a head office. They have guidelines based on gross margins by category. Suppose we had – these numbers are made up – thirty buyers. Each of them would have less than forty lines to look after. It gives them time to work with the suppliers on each line. Mastt would need a lot more buyers than that. Then you need to add the time they would waste to work out discounts, rebates and so on. It would be worse if it all had to be worked out by computer. Then staff would lose all control."

HG: "Yes, that would be a lot of hoops to jump through. If your supplier is part of your team, how do they work to create a product?"

II: "Our suppliers compete with each other when they first bid to supply us. That stops once we've made our choice. From then the supplier knows they won't be jostled out of the way by a rival. Then we can work on the teamwork. They are on the same side of the table as our buyers; they plan jointly because we all have the same aims. We stick to what we agreed to keep their goodwill and build a strong team.

"With a Mastt supplier, when the goods are on

the shelves their deal is still not done. What they get paid depends on special deals. So right up to when they pay them, it's hard to build rapport with suppliers."

All deals are special

HG: "What about discounts for bulk and so on?"

II: "None. We just have a price per unit. They send it in bulk to a regional centre, not to each store. We do all the merchandising in the store. Based on standards. We don't need point-of-sale bling. Then we pay on time. We do these things so that the supplier can make and sell us the best product. We like them to focus on that. If we don't hit sales targets then it means it's not working and we may cull that product."

HG: "I see, you don't want more discount: you want volume. All they can do is to bump up the quality. If you sell more, you both win. If you don't, you both lose. Either way, the shopper wins."

II: "The shopper has to win. Every penny they spend is theirs and their choice to spend. It's like a vote for the product they buy. The job of the supplier is to give shoppers what they want, through us. Our job is to get rid of any snags that block or slow it up.

"If a rival can do better than us, then they get the sale. And we may lose the customer. It might not be like that to start with, but that's how it will end. When shoppers have the power to push down prices they do.

"We sell a big range of basic goods. As their real prices fall, poverty falls. It's not because shoppers have a deep and profound belief in reducing poverty: it's that they like to pay less if they can. As grocers, we can go with this flow or drown [4]."

HG: "The main point is that you get suppliers to compete early in the process. You force them to focus on the spec. Then you hold them to it. They know that's how you work so they face the money issues from the start. They give you their best price first because they know you won't diddle them at the end. Once you have two thousand stores, suppliers will chase you hard for deals. They will feel the pressure on their national brands from all sides. No matter who they are, they could hedge their bets by making store brands for you.

"With Mastt, suppliers have more work to do. They must bid against their rivals for the best shelf space. All the time. Then they need to juggle with rebates, which may harm sales of products that might have done better if judged on their merits."

II: "We look after our suppliers. But we need to meet our sales targets."

TOPIC 45 NOTES

[1] See en.wikipedia. org/ wiki/ Halo_effect
[2] See also international supermarket news. com/ news/ 23057
[3] Roger Fisher & William Ury, 'Getting to Yes: Negotiating an Agreement without giving in' (UK: Random House Business Books, 1999/1981).
[4] Food prices have fallen in the last four years: theguardian .com/ money/ 2016/ may/ 07/ surprising-fall-cost-food-uk-eggs-bread-meat. However, this has not quite made up for the fall in real wages since 2008.

Topic 46: Long tail: 1996

ILLIAD CASE STUDY (fiction). Excerpt of a meeting between Illy and Homer in May 1996.

HG: "You have a small range of products. Does this cost you much in lost sales?"

II: "That is a trade-off that any store group has to make. There is a long tail effect when you stock a wide range [1]. If we gave shoppers 10pc more choice we might need 50pc more floor space. The shopper may want one more item, but it differs for each shopper. And if you serve one you must serve all.

"There are two ways to test the claim that our lost sales cost us too much. One is the number of items in a shopping basket. The other is how much is spent on each basket. We do much the same as Mastt on both of these tests. This suggests that our lost sales don't cost us too much.

"But we also sell a lot of impulse lines. Just not all at the same time. We change them each week. That adds up to a lot of SKUs in a year.

"Mastt wants to be known as a one-stop shopping store. Well, we don't. We want to be known as a one-mood shopping store. Mastt's out-of-town stores get a lot of captive shoppers. One of these days shoppers may get tired of shopping all in one go. With us they can treat their supermarket shopping as a quick in-out. Just like the old days."

HG: "There's bound to come a time when IT is so cheap that most stores will have it. They could all have the same wide range and real-time info."

II: "Sure. But we can't tell from here. For all we know, this internet thingy will wipe away Mastt's lead. Mastt may find they have too many lines with nothing to do with the supermarket as we know it. By then they may have lost their lead.

"You can't say for sure how wide your scope should be. At Illiad we focus on basic goods. So we keep a narrow product range. But we think that those who shop for basics look for the same sort of stuff. So our target market is wide. We sell to all types, when they are in the mood to shop for basics.

"When we first chose our scope in this way, we made our stores small and this helped our shoppers to shop fast. Those two things – narrow range and small size – just happened to kill running costs. We have to hold fast to that thought. Time and again, we are tempted to extend our range, to get extra sales from each shopper. We just have to make sure that we don't move too far from the ideas of small size and narrow range. Or else we may lose our edge, that is, of being cheap and fast.

"So I would say, yes, we lose a bit from the long tail effect. But what we gain from that is much more focus, which I think has more value in our sector."

HG: "As time goes by you may need to grow your range to catch the more well-off type. They also like to shop fast. But they treat some luxury goods as if they were basic goods. Such as deli items from abroad and posh ready meals."

II: "It's far too early to grow our range. The time may be ripe in a decade or two. When we reach a tipping point with our market share, say 5pc. As long as we don't stretch too far with our scope and lose focus."

HG: "Once you stretch your scope, then you can start to say that you're being disruptive. As you broaden your product range, you'll get shoppers from up and down the income scale. From then on you can fine-tune it. You can roll it out, up to two thousand stores and more. You may find a lot more than 20pc of shoppers are why-pay-more types."

TOPIC 46 NOTES

[1] *See Chris Anderson, 'The Longer Long Tail: How Endless Choice is Creating Unlimited Demand' (London: Random House Business Books, 2009).*

Topic 47: EDLP vs Bogoff

EACH INDUSTRY HAS its own set of costs. We can split an industry into segments. The scope of a segment tells us what products are sold and who its customers are. Each segment has its own set of costs.

Common sense tells us that to charge low prices and still make a profit the firm must have low costs. So the firm with the lowest costs in a segment can charge the lowest prices. If they do, they are its low-cost leader. Common sense and strategists say the same thing [1].

Any firm can do EDLP. But only one firm can be the low-cost leader: they have to have a cost edge that the rest can't match. But what if there is no low-cost leader in a segment? It should not surprise us. If one firm can buy stock at a lower cost, then the rest should be able to do the same. If one firm can pay less rent or wages, then they should all be able to.

We know that this last point has all been blown away by the notions of 'keep it small and speed it up', but we can put that aside for the time being.

A firm does not need to be the low-cost leader in their segment to do EDLP. But it would be wise not to bluff that they are the low-cost leaders. They may be found out. The shopper often shops weekly or more often, so they can't all be fooled all the time. Yet when stores stock more of their own store brands, it's harder to see who the like-for-like low-cost leader is.

If shoppers start to doubt the store's claim that they do EDLP, they may turn against the store. At least at a rival store they can get a bogof or HLP fix.

A store might not want to do EDLP and can't or does not want to be the low-cost leader. For them, bogof/ HLP may be the best bet. The risk with bogof is that the shopper might think the store is trying to outwit them. If doubt enters the shopper's mind they might seek the comfort of an EDLP store.

If a store group meets their claim – it may be EDLP or HLP with bogofs – they get one reward that can't be beat. Their shoppers learn to trust them.

The trust of their customers is the main asset of a retail firm. It acts like a bridge between two transactions, now and the next time. It's not the same as faith. As Bertrand Russell put it, faith is the 'firm belief in something for which there is no evidence' [2]. Faith has its place, but not in a retail firm. Trust is based on evidence. It grows each week, step by step, deal by deal. Like a fingernail, it grows with time – not money. But while it takes a long time to grow, trust can disappear fast.

A store group can be a low-cost leader if it changes its scope and focuses on its new segment. We know that the Big Four and the Small Two are not in the exact same segment. The scope of the Big Four is 'industry-wide.' It's broader than the Small Two, in the range of goods they sell and the shoppers they sell to.

In the UK, the strategies of the Small Two (Lidl and Aldi) don't seem to clash. So far, it's as if they were not rivals. This may be because they aren't in quite the same segment. You want a few national brands? Go to Lidl. You don't care about national brands? Go to Aldi. It's as if each is the low-cost leader in its own segment. They may be rivals but they each have their own edge.

Could one of the Big Four ignore the Small Two, do EDLP, and claim to be the low-cost leader of the Big Four? They would still define their scope as industry-wide, even if their range is wider than that. Why not? But only one of the four can be The One. Who will that One be? And what will the other three do? This may be where the sector is headed. It may have even begun. The main battle to survive might not be between the Big Four and Small Two. It might be within the Big Four. We could do some sums on their market share (see Topic 10): it's clear that at least one of them may be out of the Big Four by 2020.

Sidebar

Bogofs and HLP can be a good deal for the shopper, the retailer and the supplier.

A store in a sector with low gross margins (such as groceries) faces a big snag when it comes to pricing. They can't afford to give half-price deals. A firm with high gross margins can afford to give half-price deals. That's the type of firm a store should team up with.

It just so happens that the big FMCG suppliers are such firms. They have high fixed costs and low cost of sales. Low cost of sales means high gross margins. Now and then one of these firms may find that it has some spare capacity. They can use it to make an extra batch of one of their national brands. Their fixed costs will have been paid for at this stage. Thus the cost of the extra batch is simply its 'cost of sales' [3]. Which we know is low. The FMCG firm can sell the batch to a re-tail store group at a one-off low price. In turn, the retail store group can sell the goods in this batch on their bogof deals.

That's how the bogof deal can make sense for a grocery store and their supplier. That kind of bogof deal can also give real value to a shopper. Let's say they know the usual price of a product, which means they know if it's a good deal. If so, and the product is not perishable, the shopper can stock up. They can buy as much as will last them until they think it might next be on a bogof deal: say six months. In a short time, this should trim their shopping bills.

There is a snag for a store that does bogofs. They may find it hard to work out all the products for which a bogof deal can act as substitutes. This means the store may find it hard to work out the effect of a bogof sale on their gross margins. In turn, this may make it hard for them to plan. This may be one of the best reasons for a store to avoid bogofs. Much of what has been said about bogofs applies to HLP.

[In 2016, at least one store group cut bogofs [4].]

TOPIC 47 NOTES

[1] See en.wikipedia. org/ wiki/ Cost_leadership
[2] The 14th quote: notable-quotes. com/ r/ russell_bertrand_iii
[3] See www.accountingtools. com/ questions-and-answers/ what-is-marginal-cost.html
[4] See: dailymail.co. uk/ news/ article-3442252/ Sainsbury-s-supermarket-axe-bogof-deals-research-confusing-shoppers-actually-spend-1-274-year.

Topic 48: The public company

BASED ON WHAT they write in the media, one might think that the UK is a land of big business, with a large state and welfare sector. The fact is that we are also a nation of small firms. More than one in five people who work are business owners, mainly of small firms: they may not make much fuss but these firms produce half our goods and services.

It is common to compare the state with the private sector. But the state is the shrimp: only one sixth of people work for it. I would like to look in more depth at the goliath, where most people work: the private sector.

Here are some round figures. As of June 2016, 32 million people work in the UK. Half of them work for private firms, a third of them work for public firms, and a sixth work for the state.

The first point to note is that half the people who work (16m) do so in small to medium-sized private firms: these are firms with up to 250 staff. There are more than five million of these firms. More than 99pc of them have fewer than ten staff. Some of the owners are free-lance sole traders. It may be that some of the firms are just a shield; they are used by an employee of some other firm to cut their personal tax bill. But most of them are real firms that are run by their owners. Nearly a third of them have been made into (private) companies. And nearly a quarter of these firms have staff other than their owners. Their total sales are a bit less than half the total sales of all firms.

The second point to note is that a third of people

who work (10m) do so for large firms: they are firms with 250 or more staff. There are some 7000 of these firms in the UK. Most of them are public companies. Their total sales are a bit more than half the total sales of all firms.

The third point to note is that just a sixth of people work for the state [1].

I always use the term 'state sector' rather than 'public sector'; and I always use the term 'state ownership' rather than 'public ownership'. This is so as not to confuse a state enterprise with a public company.

Companies in the private sector may be private or public.

In law, a 'person' can be a person or a company or a firm. One way for a person to become an owner is to buy shares in a company. To buy shares in a private company, the person has to have an invite from the other owners. Most of these firms are owner-run.

Some owners of private firms choose to 'go public' at some stage. That is, they form a public company (plc) and offer some shares for sale to the public. Any person can own shares in a plc. Why and when do private firms go public? The firm may need to raise a lot of cash to expand. Or the founders may want some of that cash. Or they may want their firm to be in the public eye; going public may be a way to attract customers. Most plcs are listed on a stock exchange. That makes it easier to buy or sell its shares at a known price.

The main snag in all this is that founders might have to hand over control of their firms. Often, they then have to do as they are told.

How it all started

Why did firms need to raise cash in the first place?

In the early stage of development in a country, most work is done in the first or primary sector. People take goods from the sea or earth – they fish, mine and farm. They need cash to buy land, land rights and equipment. Land and capital are the scarce factors.

In the next stage, more work is done in the second or secondary (or manufacturing) sector. People add value to some goods to make other goods. Cash is needed to buy equipment. Capital is the scarce factor.

In the third stage, most work is done in the third or tertiary (or services) sector. This is where people provide services (and/or goods) to others. They don't need much equipment, so they don't need much cash. People's knowledge and skills are the scarce factors.

As any country develops, it shifts its focus from one sector to the next. At first it has little capital or skills, so it works mainly in the first sector. As it builds up capital, and people learn special skills, it works more in the second sector. As people become more skilled, more work start to take place in the third sector.

Goods made by adding value are priced higher than goods taken from the ground. And services done by people who use their skills are priced higher than goods that are made [2]. Some think that a country should keep a foothold in all three sectors, so it can thrive on its own if things go wrong in the world.

As long as land and capital were the scarce factors, owners had to raise cash from others. They'd raise what they could from family and friends. If that wasn't enough they'd need to raise the rest from the public.

How it all changed

Some founders no longer ran the firm once it had gone public. The Companies Act from the 1850s [3] was such that they did not have to. The firm could be run by a new breed who did not own it, called 'managers'. They have played a key role in the workforce ever since. As there was no limit to the number of managers, a firm could grow to any size. From then on, change took place fast. The number and size of firms shot up, and this fuelled the demand for managers.

In some ways to own shares in a plc is like a democracy. You may not want to vote on every issue: the managers act on your behalf. They won't do all the things you would have liked but it may be enough for you to vote for them again. If you have shares in a plc and you don't like what they do, you can sell your shares.

In plcs, managers act like agents of the owners. If there are just a few owners, they can keep an eye on the managers. Their own money is at risk and they may want to check the big decisions. But if there are thousands of owners then none of them has much say. Owners come to count on their managers more and more. Even as they start to trust them less and less. Can you trust someone else with your cash? No? This is part of what is known as 'the agency problem' [4].

These days, most large firms are plcs, with many owners. Most of these firms are run by managers. One can class these firms as 'corporates'. On average their staff earn more than the staff of private firms.

Some say that the main way that the two types of firm (private and public) differ is not based on size, but on who runs it. Most private firms are owner-run. In a plc, managers run it but don't own it, or they own a tiny share. The rise of trained managers has made for huge growth, but the agency problem is still the main snag.

Other things have changed, too.

Most firms that provide services (like retail) don't need much capital. The founders might not want to sell out or go public. Many of them have learnt how to manage. It means they can run their own firms and grow it on their own terms.

It may not work the other way round. Not many managers think like owners. Why not? Because the way to think like an owner is to be one. Not to imagine that you are one. This may be because owners have 'skin in the game' [5]. They stand to lose what they started with. This might not be the case with managers who are given shares or options to buy shares. These are seen as perks. So it might not be as easy for a plc to go back to being private, unless the founder returns, as was the case with Dell [6].

The two things that have changed the most are that services firms – which don't need much capital – now play a big role in the economy. And founders now know – they have learnt – how to manage. These changes mean that the role of the corporates has shrunk [7].

In the next few decades we may see more and more large owner-run firms, where the founders don't need or want to go public. Some of them will be family firms. Some will fail through nepotism and some will thrive. Growth will take place in and outside of the West. And more and more of these giant firms will come from Asia [8].

There are a few learning points tucked away in this topic. One: service firms – like retail – should not need to have much capital. Two: founders can learn what they need to know about managing just like anyone else. Three: if founders don't need to look for outside capital they don't need to go public, and can just run their firms the way they see fit.

But are there any pros to staying private? That's what we look at in the next topic. Note that the Big Four are plcs and the Small Two are private.

Sidebar

In some service firms – as in the case of some tech giants – the founders have the usual reasons for going public, but they don't like the loss of control. Thus most of the shares they issue to the public are non-voting. Then they run the firm as before. The public shareholders have no votes, but go along for the ride.

These cases are rare and most are recent.

TOPIC 48 NOTES

[1] From 'Here are some round figures...': 'the state' includes local and national government and public corporations. See: ons.gov. uk/ employment and labour market/ people in work/ employment and employee types/ bulletins/ uk labour market/ september 2016 # public- and- private- sector-employment and gov. uk/ government/ uploads/ system/ uploads/ attachment_ data/ file/ 467443/ bpe _2015 _statistical _release. pdf and research briefings. files. parlia-

ment.uk/ documents/ SN06152/ SN06152.pdf

[2] In the 1840s, one in five working people worked in farming and fishing; by 2011, it was less than one in a hundred. From the 1870s, slightly more people worked in services than in manufacturing. From the 1960s, services began to pull ahead fast. By 2011, eight out of ten workers worked in services; one worked in manufacturing. See webarchive. national archives. gov. uk/ 20160105160709/ and ons.gov. uk/ ons/ rel/ census/ 2011-census-analysis/ 170-years-of-industry/ sty-170-years-of-labour-market-change

[3] See en.wikipedia. org/ wiki/ Joint_ Stock_ Companies_ Act_ 1856

[4] See en.wikipedia. org/ wiki/ Principal-agent_ problem

[5] They risk their own skin, that is, their own selves in the venture. See also nytimes. com/ 2006/ 09/ 17/ magazine/ 17wwln_ safire

[6] See also the Wall Street Journal's interview with Michael Dell: wsj. com/ articles/ michael-dell-going-private-is-paying-off-for-dell-1416872851

[7] See "Are listed companies an endangered species?" at ft. com/ cms/ s/ 2/ e9f 04072-4d6c-11e4-bf60-00144 feab7de.

[8] Some 15% of American firms in the Fortune 500 are family firms; some 40% of big listed companies in Europe are family firms. McKinsey has been quoted as saying that, in 2010, 16% of large firms (over a billion dollars in sales) were owned by families from the emerging world; and that it may be 37% by 2025. See: economist. com/ news/ leaders/ 21629376-there-are-important-lessons-be-learnt-surprising-resilience-family-firms-relative?

Topic 49: Private firms: 1997

ILLIAD CASE STUDY (fiction). Excerpt of a meeting between Illy and Homer in June 1997.

HG: "Yours is a good example of an owner-run firm. I take it that you've never had the need to raise money from the outside? So there's been no need to go public? In what ways has this been a good thing?"

II: "I can speak for our firm, not for others [1]. We can focus on shopper value, not on shareholder demands. We can take a long-term view. We can afford to be risk-averse. We don't have to tell the world how we run the firm. We can work by stealth."

HG: "Why do plcs tend to focus on the short term?"

II: "Their main shareholders are fund managers. Some of them like to say that they invest for the long term. But in practice the firms in which they invest have to act in the short term. If profit doesn't grow fast enough the fund managers sell the shares and buy others. They don't care about the long term of any one firm. Why should they? They care about their own long term, which is why they'll switch at will. If other fund managers do the same, then the firm's share price falls.

"Fund managers expect a firm's profits to grow at least as fast as they have in the past. They use the share price and profits to work out what the firm is worth. They think the share price reflects all that is known about a firm at that time; so they just need to look at the price and how much it jumps up and down compared to other similar firms [2]. The share price reacts to changes in short-term profits. If profits don't grow as fast as they have in the past, the share price may drop. That's why the CEO has to base what their firm does on how it will change the share price right then.

"The irony is that in terms of their beliefs it's right for the fund managers to judge it all on share price. It is how they've been taught. But we don't have to let outsiders tell us what to do. We choose and then we do.

"We don't care if profits fluctuate in the short term. We judge what's best for our firm; we don't have to judge what's best for others. There are three things we can do much better than they can. One: we are close to the action so we can see what needs to be done. Two: we can choose what to do because we own the firm. Three: we can carry out our choices because we run the firm.

"When it's not their own cash, it's a risk for the fund managers to use their own judgement. They are blamed if they guess wrong. So they avoid that risk."

Punters or bookies

HG: "So, do you say it's like a horse-race: fund managers are like the punters?"

II: "Not quite. Sure, it's like a horse-race: but the fund managers are like the bookies. A good bookie makes money no matter which horse wins. The good bookie hedges or covers all their bets. The punters are the ones who bet. Punters are the ones who stand to lose their cash if they bet wrong.

"A fund manager earns fees. Most of their fees

are based on the amount of funds that they manage. The more punters they have on board – such as pension funds and other investors – the more fees they earn. So the main job of the fund manager is to convince punters to place their funds – to bet – with them.

"As I said, we can rely on them to think this way. We don't mind what they call it as long as they keep on doing it. It's all a part of why we keep our edge."

HG: "You talk as if decisions made for the long term are better than those made for the short term. Why's that?"

II: "I don't think that. Some decisions have to do with the long term and some with the short term. We don't care if they take years to come to fruition. We judge on what we think will be the best outcome.

"Not so with a plc. It makes sense for the fund managers to weigh up what they think will be the effect on share price in the short term. Then they hold or sell the shares. In that way they act as a financial judge. Even if they don't know much about what the firm does.

"No one can predict what will happen in the future, let alone the long term. If a firm can show gains in the short term, they think, why take a risk on the long term? So there are choices in the long term that a CEO can't even look at. That leaves an open goal for us to think long-term.

"Also, we don't need to pay dividends. One year we pay, and the next year we don't. We choose how much 'discount' we give to shoppers, and how fast we want to grow.

"Most of the time we grow using just our profits. We don't need to use financial shenanigans. For instance we don't need to shift our profits from one year to the next so as to show smooth growth [3]."

HG: "What's wrong with doing that, apart from when it's against the law?"

II: "They have to show smooth growth or their share price suffers. For us it would just be a waste of time, and it might force us to make poor decisions.

"The next thing is that we don't have the same view about debt. Many firms can grow fast if they take on debt to get some financial gearing. This is fine when things are going well. But there are risks. They can grow too fast, which can harm their image. Or there may be a downturn in the market. Negative gearing can cause huge losses. Or the accountants start to run the firm instead of the grocers. They may lose touch with what is going on in the stores. We don't like to lose touch.

What's the rush?

"Services firms like ours should not need much by way of fixed assets. That means we should not be highly geared. Low gearing means low interest cost. We can stay lean and keep fixed costs and our breakeven point low. It's not so hard to put up with a sharp recession.

"Plcs take on debt to grow fast. They have fund managers at their heels baying for faster growth. In that respect, all plc CEOs are poodles. We don't need to grow fast, full stop. The pace at which we grow depends on what things look like at the time. We grow faster than them because we plough back our profits."

HG: "Fine. The key seems to be that you can afford to take the long view. Tell me: in what ways is your being risk-averse a good thing?"

II: "We make most of our decisions in the same way as do plcs. How much can we gain from doing something, and what are the odds that we'll be right or wrong? Mastt may focus more on how much they stand to gain by being right. But we give more weight to how much it'll cost us if we are wrong. So we avoid the big risks. As long as there are deals out there to be made then our way works fine in the short term and very well in the long term. And in the long term there are always good deals to be made."

HG: "Don't plcs pay their CEOs much more than they're worth?"

II: "You're quite right – we save a lot on that. It's not as bad in our sector as in others. In the UK, CEOS of plcs get paid more than 200 times the average worker instead of 30 times, as they used to. It suits the recruiters and the fund managers for CEOs to be paid huge sums: they all know that later on it's their turn. We don't have to take part in that charade: we just pay what the job's worth to us. We have lots of people who work for us already who would fit the bill. We hope that the rest of the market just keeps on doing it that way – it's just one more thing that lets us keep our edge."

HG: "They don't have just a few owners who care deeply about that firm and its future in the long term. But what's the flip side in this issue? When would decisions made by a plc be better than those that you'd make?"

II: "What do you think?"

HG: "Checks and balances. If you had to convince a whole lot of people before you could carry out your plans you'd be less prone to go off the rails?"

II: "That might work for them. Focus groups can help with the small things, but they are a hindrance when it comes to the big things. For us, it's what we think the shopper wants that keeps us in check. We don't serve two masters – the shopper and the share-holder. We think that if what we do works for the shop-per, profits will tag along. We don't want to risk losing our boots, because we have to wear them.

"There's one more open goal I can think of. In any firm the long term may be how much time the own-ers think they've got before they can sell their shares. In a private firm like ours that is many years from now, if ever. But in a plc a new CEO may get a bonus for how much the share price goes up while they are there. If they work there for five years, that's the longest time they'll have to wait. But some of them can start to cash in after just one year in the job. Their rewards depend on the share price. That affects the type of decisions they make now. Once more we score."

TOPIC 49 NOTES

[1] See also Topic 48, Note [6]: Interview with Michael Dell by Wall Street Journal, 24th November 2014.
[2] See also en.wikipedia. org/ wiki/ Efficient-market_ hypothesis
[3] Howard Schilit, 'Financial Shenanigans' (USA: McGraw-Hill, Revised Edition, 2002), Part Two.

Topic 50: Stealth mode: 2014

ILLIAD CASE STUDY (fiction). Excerpt of a meeting between Illy and Homer in March 2014.

HG: "How much does it help you to be able to work in stealth mode?"

II: "When a rival makes a smart move we can spot it right away. It's because of the way share markets work. When the CEO explains why their profits are what they are, some of it has to be made public. The cat is out of the bag. None of this applies to private firms like ours. We don't have to make our plans public."

HG: "Okay, but how does that help?"

II: "We can do what we like without fear that Mastt will try to copy us and cause prices to go up, or undercut us. Either way it gives us a head start. We don't have to guess what they might do in response, and for them it's too late to matter.

"Mastt doesn't care about small rivals. They only began to notice us when we got close to 5pc market share. Until then, when Mastt made a fuss in the press they were quick to dismiss us. They never used to react even though they must have seen what a high growth rate we had.

"In this sector most large firms are public. A large private firm can make bold moves and the rest won't spot it. This has been the case with us. It may change as our market share gets to 5pc."

HG: "You reckon that you can work in stealth mode right up to then? How easy will it be for you to spot when they've rumbled you?"

II: "They believe in more and bigger sites out of town. We believe in small sites in built up areas, and that the big sites will be a burden in a few years. So now we wait and see. Let's say that one day Mastt says they won't buy any more new sites, and they shelve plans to build on vacant sites that they own. This would tell us that the penny has dropped. It would have dawned on Mastt that large size is the problem, not the solution. Then we would move out of stealth mode, speed up our own plans, increase TV ads and announce plans to double our store count. I think it will happen in the next few years."

HG: "Why should you drop the mask at all?"

II: "Why keep the mask on if they've seen through it? We will have lost our first mover lead. To get twice our market share we need twice the number of stores. We would prefer that our rivals don't bid for the same sites. This is one reason we didn't shout the odds. In the meantime we can add new sites and have no fear that pesky rivals might butt in.

"Once one of the Mastt firms changes tack, the rest of them will do the same. They're all scared that the rest of the gang will get ahead of them."

HG: "It's like the joke about the peckish lion that pitches up at your campfire. It's best to run like hell. You can't outrun the lion but you might outrun your friends. Mastt stores just have to beat each other.

"So why would you want to go high profile?"

II: "It may dent the morale at Mastt. It may cause more shoppers to be curious about us. And, when they see our TV ads, more shoppers may drop in on our stores.

"It's fine for our firm to have a high profile, but not fine for our staff. Owners like me who don't need to be in the public eye go out of their way to avoid it. Most people in Illiad don't know what I look like. They know who our CEO is in each country. But we prefer that they too keep a low profile. It must be a total bore to be in the public eye. CEOs at plcs aren't so lucky. They need to defend their actions and be admired. This can waste a lot of time. And it might not work."

CHAPTER 8: GROWTH

Topic 51: Making space

A STORE MAY decide to add more floor space to the stores they have at the moment or to add more stores. There are two aspects to this type of decision. The first is that it is financial. The firm aims to spend a large sum to earn more profit each year in the future. The second is that it is strategic. It commits the firm to do things in a specific way for years.

The strategic aspect can cost them more if it turns out to have been the wrong decision. In retail, sales depend in a large part on where they locate their store. So it can be quite high risk. It may not seem to be high risk in financial terms. The numbers can look good, and they can be made to look better the further ahead we look. But it can be high risk in strategic terms. A lot of things can change the pattern of demand, so it makes more sense to commit to only a few years ahead.

How far ahead it is safe to look depends on what kind of business they are in. They need to look far ahead in the steel business, but not too far ahead if they are a retail firm.

One might think that demand and supply of floor space is not hard to work out. Both can be measured in square feet (or metres). From there one should be able to tell if a sector has spare space. But demand and supply are not so easy to match. Vacant space might not be a sign of too much capacity. Some vacancies may be due to churn. Then there's the actual use to which the space is put. There may be a dearth of one type or size of site, and a glut of another. One should compare like with like. Supply may go up if all firms plan to grow at the same time: and they don't compare notes. A dearth can change to a glut all at once.

Over time, supply and demand should stay more or less in sync. The market price of space – rent – sees to that. It will do so as long as the market is free to sort out mismatches. But this can be costly. For instance, say a store has to change from being a retail store to an online fulfilment warehouse. The market rent and hence price of the property would fall sharply.

From 1995, sales in the grocery sector grew at close to 2pc each year. Then, in mid-2009, sales growth stopped: and that's the way it stayed [1]. Supply is now far more than demand.

Some experts have a good grasp of what the risks are to the Big Four, but they don't say much. Still, some have said that the floor space in this sector should fall by a fifth; sales could fall by 3pc per year in the six years to 2020; if put to residential use sites could halve in value; and some food retailers might not survive [2].

It should be clear that if demand stays more or less the same for the next few years then grocery firms should not open more stores. They should shrink in both size and number. Yet both Aldi and Lidl plan to double their store count in the next few years. That means they would need to take market share from the rest. Will it be that easy? The answer in terms of what we've seen so far seems to be, yes, no problem. We just can't tell how much market share each of the Big Four will lose: that depends on the choices they each make.

When the Big Four went for one-stop stores they did not just change the size of the shopping space: they changed how much time was spent on a shopping trip. Shoppers had been used to shopping in small chunks of time. Then, when big stores came on the scene, shoppers bundled their time into one big weekly trip. Since the rise in small stores things may have changed again. It may have gone back to shopping little but often.

If that is the case then there are too many grocery stores, they are too big, and they may be in the wrong place. How big is this problem? And how can the Big Four deal with it? If there is a third too much space then the cost to sort it out could run into billions of pounds. That is the financial side. There is also the strategic side. If they take a few years to sort it out how much will sales suffer?

To get a feel for the scale of the problem we'll take a look at retail property in the next three topics.

TOPIC 51 NOTES

[1] See food deserts. org/ images/ supshare: nominal sales values were deflated with the Retail Price Index; from 1995 these grew by 27% in fourteen years; and by just 1% in the next five.
[2] 'Some experts have ...': See 17 November 2014: telegraph.co. uk/ finance/ news by sector/ retail and consumer/ 11235652/ Goldman-Sachs-Supermarket-groups- must-close-one-in-five-stores

Topic 52: Gearing vs leverage

THESE TWO WORDS mean the same thing. The word 'gearing' is used in the UK. The word 'leverage' is used in the USA and by some in the UK; in the USA it is pronounced to rhyme with 'beverage'.

There are two types of gearing. One is known as 'financial', and the other is known as 'operating'. The first is more well-known but the second is the one we need to know about at this stage.

Gearing affects both the balance sheet and the profit and loss account. We will only look at its effect on the latter.

Gearing gives us the ratio of fixed costs to total costs. To see how it works, we can compare the gearing of two firms. Say that the one firm is a Mastt grocery store. The other firm, X, is in some other sector. We should first compare our costs.

As before, Mastt's sales are £100k and cost of sales is £73k, so gross profit is £27k. Less fixed (running) costs of £22k means they are left with operating profit (OP) of £5k.

If sales go up by 10pc but fixed costs stay the same, by how much does OP go up? We know that the gross margin is always the same. This means that gross profit should also go up by 10pc. At present gross profit is £27k, so it will go up by £2.7k. As there's no change in fixed costs, OP will also go up by £2.7k.

Our OP was £5k. If we divide 2.7 by 5 we get 0.54. Thus OP goes up by 54pc.

To sum up: with Mastt, sales and gross profit go

up 10pc, yet OP goes up 54pc. The only extra cost is that of goods sold. The constant fixed costs act like a fulcrum so we have 'geared up' our OP.

Now let's take firm X. Sales (£100k), total costs (£95k), and the OP (£5k) are the same as for Mastt. But the fixed and variable costs – which add up to the total costs – are not the same: we say that the cost structure differs. Cost of sales is £35k, so gross profit must be £65k. Less fixed (running) costs of £60k means they are left with £5k OP.

If sales go up by 10pc but fixed costs stay the same, by how much does OP go up? We know that the gross margin is always the same. This means that gross profit should also go up by 10pc. At present gross profit is £65k, so it will go up by £6.5k. As there's no change in fixed costs, OP will also go up by £6.5k.

Our OP was £5k. If we divide 6.5 by 5 we get 1.3. Thus OP goes up by 130pc.

To sum up: in firm X, sales and gross profit go up 10pc, yet OP goes up 130pc. The only extra cost is that of goods sold. The constant fixed costs act like a fulcrum so we have 'geared up' our OP.

This shows that with a sales increase, OP goes up more with firm X than with Mastt. Firm X is said to be 'more highly geared'.

How does this work? The reason is that the ratio of fixed costs to total costs is higher for firm X than for Mastt. That is to say, variable costs for firm X are less than for Mastt. So firm X has a higher gross margin. What happens once gross profit starts to exceed fixed costs? With firm X, their extra net profit is 65pc of their sales; with Mastt, their extra net profit is just 27pc of their sales. Thus firm X makes much more profit from the extra sales than does Mastt.

For those who like graphs, the slope of the gross profit line is steeper in firm X. To reduce the chance of a muddle we can stick to our numbers and leave out the graphs. But there are some good graphs for those who like them [1].

What's the risk?
We can make two points here. Gearing boosts a firm's OP by a greater percentage than its rise in gross profit. And the higher the firm's gross margin the bigger the gain from gearing. This is true of any firm. Although Mastt is not highly geared, it can gain from gearing. Not as much as with firm X, but some.

Once a highly geared firm like X breaks even it makes profits fast. It makes lots of gross profit and hence lots of OP for each pound in extra sales. But if it falls below break-even it makes losses fast, for the same reason. Thus, with high gearing, the firm makes a high reward for a high risk. What risk? The risk is that they run out of cash in tough times. That is, the risk is that they go bust.

When managers make a choice that will cause gearing to go up, they ought to know that risk will go up. Before they go ahead they ought to work out what the cost will be if things go wrong.

Say we were to think about the risks of starting a new firm. We may have to commit to some fixed costs. For how long? To rent premises we might have to sign a lease for at least three years. With wages we might allow for a few months. To work out the risk, we'd add it all up to look at the worst case. We'd want to know how much cash we'd need to have before we start. Just in case we have low sales for longer than we thought. Our fixed costs have to be paid no matter what.

Which type of cost is more risky? We know that (variable) cost of sales only come to pass if and when we have sales. Let's say we have no fixed costs. If we have no sales we don't risk running out of cash. Whereas when we commit to fixed costs we do risk running out of cash. Even if a firm with lots of assets runs out of cash it can still go bust, fast.

What rules of thumb should we use when we want to increase sales?

If we can do so without a rise in costs, fine. If not, we should try to make sure that they are only variable. At least to start with, until we find out if sales go up like we thought they would. But if fixed costs have to rise, well, perhaps we need to weigh it up a bit more. Do we have the cash reserves in case sales don't go up?

A sector with low gearing has less to gain. So before we raise our fixed costs we should weigh it up with more care in the groceries sector.

The same rules of thumb should apply when we want to grow a firm. One way to increase sales might be to add floor space. Fixed costs will go up, by rent or interest, and perhaps wages. OP would go up if the extra gross profit is more than the extra fixed (running) costs. Risk will increase. Does that matter? Well, risk starts to matter when sales fall.

A matter of timing

In the nineties the market leaders opened more and

bigger stores. Their profits would have gone up. They would have known that sales and floor space were linked. And they would have known that sales could not grow much more than the rate of growth in population. Even if wages grew and there was more cash to spend.

For sales to keep going up, stores would have to sell a wider range of goods. They did not need to stick with groceries. Gross margins on some of these new lines might have been more than those on groceries. It might have pushed up their gross margin as a whole.

In this way they would have kept the link between sales and floor space. We know that they opened more stores. Their profits kept on going up.

From 2003 to 2008 one of the Big Four store groups boosted their floor space by 50pc. By 2015 they had boosted it once more by 50pc. This store group had nearly twice as many stores in 2015 as in 2003 [2].

After the banking crash in 2008, did the Big Four think that growth might slow down? Or did they think that growth would keep on going up? What did they think might happen if growth stopped?

Then growth stopped. That's when the bad news began. Slowly at first. Since then, the Big Four have lost market share. The Small Two gained that market share but at first it was too small to notice. It was noticed once it reached a combined 5pc, which was where our story began. Now the Big Four face the same problems as they did then. Just bigger.

The Big Four still have to deal with rivals in the non-grocery sector. Some of these rivals are online, where prices are keen. This will have cut short one of the Big Four's growth routes. Apart from this point, I have ignored online firms as they play no direct role in the wars between the Big Four and Small Two. From 2020 they may play more of a role in this sector than they do now (see Topic 57).

We know that the Small Two intend to grow their store count. Based on what we've said so far, their sales should grow at least at the same rate as they are doing now. But if there is no sales growth in the sector as a whole then the sales of the Big Four would have to fall.

The main snag for the Big Four would be if their fixed costs failed to fall in sync with their fall in sales. We know that it's hard to cut fixed costs. The hardest costs to cut are those in respect of floor space. The costs of rent or interest on debt can't be cut in the short term.

This brings us back to the issues of risk and gearing. In the quest for growth, it may be that the Big Four piled on fixed costs. This would have stepped up their risk. When fixed costs are high and sales fall then reverse gearing kicks in. Each plus during the growth phase turns into a minus. If profit grows faster than the rest in an up phase, it will fall faster than the rest in a down phase.

Based on this topic, there are at least two rules of thumb that may work for the Big Four in the next six years. They should cut their fixed costs by more than their fall in gross profit. And they should convert more of their fixed costs to variable costs.

Earlier, we looked at some of the risks of big price cuts. Yet the Big Four may try to cut prices to throw their rivals off the scent, or to signal to their core shoppers that they are taking bold action. But these tactics will wear thin quite fast if they run out of cash.

The first two rules of thumb above may work for a while. They might bring down the break-even point of these firms so they can survive on lower sales. It might even give them time to work out a new strategy.

In the next topic we look at how to work out the cost of reverse gearing. Then we ask if there are ways for the Big Four to be better prepared to deal with the fall in sales than we've seen so far.

Sidebar

Sales may rise quite a bit before fixed costs rise. I assumed that, despite a ten per cent rise in sales, fixed costs would stay more or less the same.

High operating gearing is where OP fluctuates more than gross profit. This is due to high fixed running (operating) costs.

High financial gearing is where net profit fluctuates more than OP. This is due to high fixed interest costs.

In both cases the firm is at risk when it is highly geared and sales fall. The big risk is that they run out of cash. The worst risk is when the firm uses both types of gearing at the same time, and sales fall.

TOPIC 52 NOTES

[1] See also accountingtools. com/ operating-leverage
[2] See also telegraph.co. uk/ business/ 2016/ 09/ 11/ tesco-chairman-the-supermarket-space-race-is-to-blame-for-many-o

Topic 53: Reverse gearing

WAS IT A good idea for the Big Four to increase their floor space and move out of town? We have seen why they would have been tempted to do so. It might have seemed like a numbers game. There would have been no need to know about the grocery business. It's all about the link between floor space and sales.

From their point of view, more floor space would let them broaden their scope. They could then go for a wider range of products and shoppers. That could push up sales and gross margins. To keep rent low, they could get out of town and turn their stores into destination stores.

On the downside, the worst case would be if sales were to fall. They would need to work out the risk of reverse gearing. To do so, they would have to answer a simple question. 'By how much would sales need to fall for us to lose all of our profit?' A quick way to work this out is to turn the gross margin into a ratio, then divide the fall in profit by the ratio.

Say that sales are £100k, operating profit (OP) is £5k, and gross margin is 27pc (or .27). By how much would sales need to fall for them to lose their OP of £5k?

If we divide 5 by .27 we get 18.5. We must subtract this from 100. Thus if sales fell from £100k to £81.5k they would lose their OP of £5k [1].

That's a fall in sales of nearly 20pc – not a bad safety margin [2]. It shows that if sales fall, OP doesn't fall as fast as it would if they cut selling prices. So they would have more time to act. But it may be too late if they also cut their selling prices.

Reverse gearing is just one of the downsides they would have looked at. They might also have looked at the strategic downside. A strategic choice binds one for the long-term. For each such choice they would have worked out the cost of it not working out.

In the year 1995 what could the Big Four have foreseen about the market today? Say we look at what took place in the market to get where it is now. How could the store groups have known these things would take place? How could they have known that an internet would come from nowhere?

Let's say that our answer is, no, they could not have foreseen any of that; nor should we expect them to have done so. No one can work out the odds of what might happen in an unknown future; if you don't know what it is how can you work out the odds of it taking place? Let alone those things you know about that might not take place.

Can we say that in the light of what they ought to have known then that their choices were poor? Say we look at it from the vantage point of 1995. We might conclude that there was no flaw in their strategy, or in their numbers. That is, based on what they ought to have known, they made sound choices. What they did worked for more than a decade, and was admired all over the world.

No blame

So where's the catch? Why did things go wrong? Was it that they didn't change with the times? Or did they use a good formula for too long?

What would Christensen say? It seems that the disruptors win, as long as the market leaders do the 'right thing' [3]. Huh? He says that disruptors go for a segment with low margins and few customers. The 'right thing' for the leaders to do is to stay out of this new segment. They should rather listen to their own customers and give them more of what they want. That would be to go upmarket into segments where they could get higher gross margins. They should not go down-market into segments that are too small to count.

The irony is that in doing the right thing the leaders pave the way for the disruptors to win.

It seems that the Big Four did the right thing. They went for a broader scope than basic groceries. Yet this made the path clear for the Small Two and their small footprint stores to win with low prices.

Does this mean that Christensen would say that it had to happen this way? That even if the Big Four lose much of their market share, they did nothing wrong? And there is nothing they could have done about it? All this time they were bobbing corks who thought that they were acting on purpose?

For them not to have been mere bobbing corks they would have had to have been acting on purpose. That means they must have brought it on themselves. They must have exposed their weak flank when they went for high gross margins. For that to be true, they must have made strategic errors. What could these have been? What was their weak flank?

It might have been that the Big Four committed too far into the future. That made it too hard for them to change their business model when the time came for them to do so. If one goes deep into a maze and comes face to face with the Minotaur, what is the best that one can hope for? The ball of twine is fine: it helps one to get back to where one started [4]. But even to do that, in this case, would take years. How do they unravel a business model based on giant scale when small scale is called for? And will it cost them more than they've got? Or do they persist with what they've done, where they are, with what they've got, and face the Minotaur [5]? There are times when it's better to face it.

To recap, maybe they went so far with their strategy that they will find it hard to get back. With no spare paddles they bravely went up the creek.

There are some learning points we may pick up from this.

One: we can't be sure of our forecasts. Two: we should try to commit no further ahead than we are fairly sure of our forecast. Three: we should avoid any option where the cost of it not working out is more than the firm can bear. This could be dubbed 'don't bet the farm'. Only then should we look at the rest of the choices. Four: if sales start to fall, we should cut fixed costs more than the fall in sales. But if we can't do that, rather accept the fall in sales than slash prices.

These may be valid rules of thumb in this sector at this time. It is a mature market, with too much capacity and tight gross margins. It does not mean we can use these rules of thumb in any sector at any time.

But they may help to frame some of the property choices faced by retailers.

Sidebar

There are a few examples of how to deal with disruptors. One could look at Intel in the days when the Pentium was their star range. AMD and other firms began to disrupt this market. Intel then brought out the Celeron range. The Celeron was seen as the rival to AMD and the other firms. The Pentium is still seen as the star range. So Intel pulled it off. How they did it is a story on its own [6].

TOPIC 53 NOTES

[1] To test this, we work it out backwards. We want to check that if sales fall to £81.5 then OP is zero. If we take £81.5k times .27 we get £22k gross profit. But £22k is our running cost. If we subtract £22k (running cost) from £22k (gross profit) we get an OP of zero.

[2] See also ...accountingtools.com/ margin-of-safety

[3] See Clayton M Christensen, 'The Innovator's Dilemma' (New York: Harper Business, 1997/2003), 112-3. Among the 'right things' to do he includes: listen to customers, track competitors' actions, and focus on high-quality products that earn higher profits.

[4] See ...greece.mrdonn.org/ theseus

[5] Based on a coffee mug slogan, attributing to Teddy Roosevelt the advice 'Do what you can, where you are, with what you have.'

[6] See 'Intel's revenge': forbes. com/ 1999/ 01/ 14/ feat and 'Intel and AMD: The Juggernaut vs. The Squid': forbes. com/ sites/ rogerkay/ 2014/ 11/ 25/ intel-and-amd-the-juggernaut-vs-the-squid/

Topic 54: Penny or bun?

How can a retail firm cash in on their blue-chip status? Can they do this with property deals? Would the owner of a private firm look at it in the same way as the boss of a plc?

The market price of a property rests on if it has a tenant. If it's vacant it has a market price. If it has a tenant with a lease at market rent the market price goes up. If it's a long lease and the tenant is seen as blue-chip then the market price goes up some more.

In what way does 'value' differ from 'price'? From what I've seen, value hinges on who's doing the talking. There are lots of ways to value anything. A good negotiator gets the rest to agree on the way that most helps their own case. But the market price is how much an investor would pay when the talking stops. Are there ways to work out this market price? Yes there are. So here I use market price.

A retailer may want to own the site from which they trade. It may be that they want to stay there as long as they like. Or that they never want to have to ask an owner to let them alter the premises.

An investor wants a return on what they invest. It is based on the net rent they can get over the life of the property. They don't know the annual rate of growth in net rent in the long term. So they use a measure of the current return, known as the Yield.

Net rent is gross rent less costs that strictly 'come with the property', such as rates, insurance and maintenance. Net rent as a percentage of the market price is called the yield. Top real estate firms make known the current yields on prime and secondary property all over the world [1].

Market price is based on what is known to be the current yield on properties of that type; on its market rent; and on its current rent. If you know these three numbers you can start to work out the price an investor would pay, or at least around which the parties could negotiate.

The present value of future net rent may be worked out as a cross-check. We should note that 'yield' does not mean the same thing in both cases. Investment yield can refer to the internal rate of return (IRR) of an investment; the IRR is the rate at which the net present value of all projected cash flows is zero. On the other hand, property yield is based on actual current amounts, not projections.

The main risk to an investor is that their tenant goes bust so they don't get all the rent. A blue-chip tenant is less likely to go bust. But if they do, a new tenant is not so hard to find if it's a good property. The least risk is to have a blue-chip tenant on a long lease in a good property. The lower the risk, the lower the yield, and the higher the price.

The retailer is faced with two main issues when they look at a site. The first is for how long they are sure it would suit their shoppers. This is based on their judgement as grocers. The second is for how long they have to occupy the site. This is based on what they can negotiate. The least risk is where they can match the two. That means that they should aim to stay as long as they are sure it would suit their shoppers. One way is for them to do a sale and leaseback, where they land up as the tenant.

A smart retailer who knows that the tenant and the investor do not 'value' a site in the same way can make a quick buck.

The retailer forms a new firm to own property. The new firm buys a vacant site on which it builds premises. It can now draw up a long lease with the retailer (itself). The lease would be for a long term at market rent. The retailer now sells the new firm for a top price to an investor.

Where's the quick buck? The investor now owns premises with a blue-chip firm as tenant on a long lease. That's the kind of deal they like, so they would have paid a high price. The price would have been more than the cost to buy and build on the site in the first place. Thus the retailer would have made a profit on the deal. In effect they will have used their blue-chip status to do a deal for a high price.

If they are a plc the windfall profit will cause their share price to go up. If they do the same thing each year, their share price will keep going up.

Some may say that this is growth by financial engineering. That it's not the result of trading skills. The retail firm might say that they are using all their skills. They are grocers, not investors; they built an ideal site for their own use; they like to focus on trading; and so on. Shareholders in a plc might not mind as long as their profits go up in the short term.

Where's the catch?
The catch may be the length and terms of the lease. To

see why, we need to look at how a sale and leaseback may play out in the long term.

Demand by the Big Four for out-of-town stores went up for years. That would have pushed up the market rent for that type of property. That in turn would have pushed up its market price.

Once fewer shoppers went out of town to shop, demand for those stores would fall. That would push down the market rent for that type of property. That in turn would push down its market price.

There is a dilemma if demand falls. The retail firm may choose to stay put and pay too much rent for a number of years, or to take the knock in one go and get out. But if they stay they may lose too many shoppers and it will plague them for the rest of the lease. No matter what they do they are making a choice. That is, the actual cost if they get out now versus the profit and market share they forfeit if they don't.

Say the firm gets out of the lease, pays the costs and moves closer to town. The loss would not show up as a running cost. This means it might not reflect badly on their trading skills. But the loss would have to be shown somewhere further down. Thus it would affect their net profit and their earnings per share. The share price may drop and the board may fire the CEO.

Why would the retail firm have to take a big loss if they move out? As long as they are the tenant they have to pay the high rent. If they leave, the price of the property would fall. (It would have lost a blue-chip tenant). The investor would have made sure at the start of the lease that there was a penalty clause. This clause would have stated how much the tenant would have to pay to get out of the lease. It might cost the tenant – the retail firm – more than the total balance of rent due if they were to leave early.

Why then does the length of the lease matter? The longer the lease with a blue-chip tenant the higher the price of the property. And the more windfall profit to the retail firm at the start. But there would be more risk that the site would one day stop suiting their shoppers, and of a big loss to the retail firm.

When would it matter? When the location of the site stopped meeting the needs of shoppers. To whom would it matter? Here's the nub. It would matter to the owners of the retail firm. Retail sales might fall if they can't get out of the lease. They would not want to fall into the trap of reverse gearing. It could cost them millions or, if they had made lots of deals like this, billions.

In the case of a plc, the CEO who had done those deals may have left the firm. Their bonus would have taken into account profits from the deals. This may be one of the snags with decisions that take a long time to play out, yet where rewards are based on the short term. In contrast, in the case of an owner-run firm they have to think of the effects in the short and the long term.

Penny and bun

It is clear that unless things go wrong there are no losers in this kind of sale and leaseback. In a plc, the worst that one could say is that the CEO failed to predict the future. No blame. A CEO can expect to stay in their post for a few more years. They might not be there ten years hence. It's of no use to try and pick holes in their past choices.

We have all faced dilemmas. As with any choice we make, if it works out right we like to take full credit. And if it goes wrong we can usually find an outside cause to blame [2].

Unless we own the firm the buck is passed to the next guy.

In a sale and leaseback, is there a better way? It is tempting to think of it as an either-or issue. But it can be thought of as a both-and issue. Thus we should aim to have as long a lease as we might need, without having to commit to more than say five to eight years in one go. We'd like the least cost of exit and for it to be at our behest.

We could use our blue-chip status to get a deal with less risk. Thus we could go for a shorter lease with some options to renew. But the market price would be lower for a property with that type of lease. Investors like a long lease with no wriggle room.

So our choice is between more risk to get a higher price now, or less risk to get a lower price now. How much lower would the market price of the property be on a lease of five years versus one for twenty years? That question has to do with finance. What is the difference worth to us? That question has to do with strategy: its answer is the price we are prepared to pay to keep our options open.

If the firm were private, how would the owner view this choice? The owner hopes to own the firm for the long term. Why be in a rush? Does it matter if they get extra jam today or no jam today but jam tomorrow? Why take a needless risk?

If the retail firm owns the premises from the start they can sell it when the time is right. They don't make the quick buck that they might have done with a leaseback. But they don't risk as big a loss in the future if they want to sell early. Also, they can stay with what they're good at: being grocers. This is the long-term way. It may be the safe way.

Or we could say, if it's our own firm, why try to bring forward profits we might not earn in the future? Why pay tax on tomorrow's profit? If we guess right we'll earn it anyway, just not today. If we guess wrong it'll cost us more than we brought forward in the first place, and then some.

The right decision at the time may still turn out to be wrong. One wants to be able to backtrack if shopper habits change.

The reader may want to keep an eye on what takes place in this sector in the next few years [3].

TOPIC 54 NOTES

[1] colliers. com/- /media/ files/ emea/ uk/ research/ research%20 and%20 forecasting/ 201507-property-pricing-survey. pdf?
[2] See en.wikipedia. org/ wiki/ Self-serving_bias
[3] See also (on 23 April 2015): wsj. com/ articles/ changing-customer-habits-leave-supermarkets-with-property-dilemma-1429794380

CHAPTER 9: OPTIONS

Topic 55: Future shocks: 2015

ILLIAD CASE STUDY (fiction). Excerpt of a meeting between Illy and Homer in March 2015.

II: "Do we spend too much on TV ads? We're a retail firm, so why should we spend so much on above the line ads? Why don't we just do product ads and focus on quality and price?"

HG: "Your rivals now know that you are a threat to them. So you don't need to use stealth any more. Now you should let your shoppers know that you're here to stay. You need to sound a bit more like the rest."

II: "What if we just stayed with EDLP and kept up standards? At some stage we'd get most of the why-pay-more shoppers. Surely that should let us cut back on ads?"

HG: "You've said that the day would come when you could join the dots. Once you have enough stores to cover the whole of the UK, you'll no longer be seen as a regional group. One of these days you want it to be clear that you're a national group. Right?"

II: "Right. But we are growing at the right pace."

HG: "I think you should let the market know you're here. You may have a snag with your image. For two decades you've ploughed profits back, to grow the group. You've kept a low profile for so long that some shoppers don't know who you are. You are not some Johnny Foreigner come-lately. You want them to know that you are now more of a local firm.

"And you want more first-time shoppers in the stores. Make it easy for them to give you a try. It's an image thing. The best way to draw them in is to plug away with TV commercials."

II: "Okay, okay. Once we've got two thousand stores they can be the magnet. For now, we want shoppers who haven't done so yet to try us out.

"But what should we do when what they call austerity ends? Will shoppers start to spend too much, like before? Or will they watch the pennies? Will they still think that low price means poor quality?"

HG: "You should do the same thing no matter how the market reacts. You want to keep the why-pay-more shopper. They are your core market. They can tell the difference between price and value, and they care. Keep them happy. For now, stay focused on growing your store count. That's your key to sales growth."

Check the competition

II: "Fine. Now what don't we want Mastt to do in the next six years?"

HG: "You don't want them to change too much too fast. A big bang approach would threaten what they've got now. It's too soon. They might try and fail. It might disrupt the rest of the market. You want time to get up to two thousand stores at your own pace. It would be better if they were all to adjust slowly.

"If one of the Mastt firms went too far with their discounts they could also go bust. It would reduce floor space in the sector in one go. You'd pick up quite a bit of the trade but so would the rest of the Mastt firms. I'm not sure what the effect will be."

II: "Do you think one of them will try a big bang approach?"

HG: "Who knows? Those who learnt their lessons in the nineties won't be caught out again. But a new breed might repeat the mistakes of the past. They might be led astray. There'd be lots of consulting fees to earn."

II: "No, fine. We'd like the market to be stable. We'd prefer to take their market share from them bit by bit. At least until we get to our 20pc share. Then maybe we can speed it up. Where do you think threats will come from, apart from online?"

HG: "The market may fragment. That means more small firms. If they can keep their footprint small and their fixed costs low they should be fine. But rents and rates may be too high for them in the centres of towns and cities."

II: "I've noticed that. As more firms go online there should be less demand for space in the high street. So rents and rates should come down. But they don't. So we pay more, but have fewer rivals."

HG: "It might turn out that way. Now, Mastt stores may or may not change the way they do things, but other small firms are sure to find the gaps. Some of them may try to disrupt you like you did with Mastt. They could go for store brands in a big way right from the start. They could stock four hundred versus your fifteen hundred lines. You used to have eight hundred lines but you've let this creep up. Your secret is still the same: fast shopping and a small store with low prices. Now you want to expand your product range and your price range. Your model is still EDLP versus your rivals, so you are safe for now. But you have left a gap."

II: "A gap? What gap?"

HG: "You have shown the way – the need for speed. These new rivals could have stores of four hundred square metres, where you have twelve hundred. They could have lower fixed costs, and so be cheaper."

II: "That would be an outrage!"

HG: "Sure. But, aside from that, what do you think?"

II: "Yes, it could happen. The shopper now buys some twenty items per shop. With store of four hundred square metres, shoppers will buy less, but for them it'll still be faster and cheaper. These new firms could not replace us. But they could disrupt us. How long would it take?"

HG: "If they had none of the right stores to start with they'd need ten years to make an impact. But who knows? It's all in the future."

II: "We'll stay with what we know for now. But what if a Mastt firm tried to copy us? If they did things in the same way as us?"

HG: "I don't rate their chances because they'll be stuck for a few years with the way they do things now. You've been doing things in a tried and tested way in thousands of stores world-wide for decades. They would, more or less, have to start from scratch. It's like if nature tried to evolve a bird from scratch. At the start it may look more like a pterodactyl. To get to a bird would take quite a bit longer."

Topic 56: Hard or soft landing

WHAT CAN THE Big Four do? Will they accept that they are going to lose a big chunk of market share in the next few years, and start to deal with the real snags one step at a time? If so, they and their staff may have a soft landing. Or will they stay in denial, and refuse to accept that they are going to lose more market share? Then these firms and their staff may have a hard landing.

They could lose market share and still have a soft landing. Every year people retire or change jobs. The firms would just replace less of them. They may ease up on their intake of temps and part-time staff [1]. The job market is better than it has been for some years, which may ease the pain for those who lose their jobs. The key for the firms and staff is always the same: the firm should think ahead, and staff should keep learning new skills.

Say the Big Four need to lose a third of their staff in the next six years. This is about 5pc each year. Let's say that the staff turnover rate in the UK is not less than 15pc each year [2]. It may be much more than this in supermarkets. A firm needs to hire at least 15pc new staff each year just to stay in the same place. But say the Big Four were to hire only 10pc new staff each year. Their total staff would fall by 5pc each year and there might be little need for them to retrench.

Compare this to a big bang approach. A large number of staff may lose their jobs and the change may not even work out. More than a million people work in this sector. So if it were to shrink by a third too quickly then the cost would be high.

Each of the Big Four will deal with this in their own way. We shoppers will go on shopping in a way that suits us. The real test is what we do (where we shop), not what we think about their strategies. Every now and then we can look at the scorecard – the market share of each firm – out of interest.

No matter when it's done, the number of jobs in this sector will fall. That's the pain, so where's the gain? The real price of groceries will fall. Millions of households will have more cash to spend. If they spend 5pc less than they would have spent, it adds up to £5 billion per year. When did the state last give that much cash to shoppers?

How do we rank the pain of those who fail to get jobs that they might have got against the gains to the rest of us? Those who fail to get jobs may get jobs elsewhere. We all gain because we all buy groceries. But who amongst us will show the biggest gains?

The poorest will gain the most. That's the group that spends the highest ratio of their income on basic groceries. Real price cuts are better than a rise in wages and there's no tax to pay. Even those earning the lowest wages have to pay tax in the UK. National Insurance might not be called a tax on income, but to those who pay it, it seems like one.

To recap: this real cut in the price of groceries will be of real social benefit in the UK. It will have come from a real boost in productivity. It may be one of the best ways to give to those who have less. And in the next six years, the Big Four firms may be able to achieve a soft landing for both their firms and their staff. It might still be tough for many people, but not as tough as a hard landing.

TOPIC 56 NOTES

[1] Over half of retail staff are part-time: gov. uk/ government/ uploads/ system/ uploads/ attachment_ data/ file/ 252383/ bis-13-1204-a-strategy-for-future-retail-industry-and-government-delivering-in-partnership. pdf
[2] See hr grapevine. com/ markets/ hr/ article/ 2014-06-12-employee-turnover-rises

Topic 57: Match or tweak?

AS THINGS STAND, the Small Two are taking market share from the Big Four. Even in the long term it may be hard for the Big Four to match the Small Two on price. The Small Two are the lowest cost food retailers, and they use EDLP. They carry mainly their own store brands, and they focus on fast shopping in small stores.

The Big Four seem to have at least one strong edge. They each carry a full range of national brands.

The Big Four could stock more of their own store brands, but if they kept all their national brands they would need more floor space. To save space they could cut down their range of national brands, but this would erode their edge: they may lose some of their shoppers.

The Big Four may need to do at least three things. One, keep their range of national brands. Two, use less space. Three, stock more store brands. The snag may be that at best they can do only two of these.

Should the Big Four try to match some of the things done by the Small Two? Or should they tweak what they've got now?

To stay on as market leaders the Big Four would need to change their cost structure. To do that they'll need to change some of their key strategies. They might not be able to extend their scope like they did in the past. That is because when they began to sell non-groceries they clashed with online retail.

Low price is a key feature of online retail. It may affect the prices that the Big Five stores can charge in-store. Thus it is a real threat to the sales of non-grocery lines in-store.

How big a threat is online retail to the Big Four? It is now (August 2016) a seventh of all retail sales, and it is growing fast. At this rate, in four years it may be a quarter to a third of all retail sales. This means it could be quite a big threat to the Big Four.

How big a threat is online food retail? Food retail by itself is only a sixth of all retail. Online food retail is one twentieth of all food retail, and it's not growing fast. At this rate, in four years it may be up to one seventeenth of all food retail. So it does not yet seem to be a threat to the sales of food lines in-store. Thus it's not yet a threat to the Small Two [1].

It may have been just bad luck that the Big Four moved into non-groceries at the same time as online firms.

The upshot is that the Big Four have low-cost rivals on both sides. With online rivals on one side and the Small Two on the other they risk being cut off at the pass. If they try to play catch-up with the Small Two it's hard to see how it could take them less than six years. They'd need to change or add 1500 stores of the right size just to match them. Why should the Big Four bother? There's been no sign that they'd like to be in the small footprint retail market. Yet if they want to sell basic groceries they are going to have to do it on price. Not only, but at least on price. The shopper won't keep paying a third more for a few loyalty card points.

The real price of most goods has come down for some two hundred years [2]. Once a certain standard is reached with any goods, they start to get cheaper. We should recall that Porter says that if you can't be the cheapest you have to be different; Christensen adds that if you can't be different, make it cheaper or someone else will [3].

The Big Four should aim to make their groceries seem to differ from (and be better than) those sold by the Small Two. They can then charge more and the shopper who likes them will buy them. The Small Two should aim to make their groceries seem to be the same as those sold by the Big Four. They can then charge less and shoppers will buy them because they are cheaper.

To make goods that are – or seem to be – different a firm needs to think of new things. How does a store 'invent' new grocery lines? They might add value with no change in price; or take things away with no change in quality; or reduce the space it takes up, such as with smart packaging.

Christensen says that the best way for leaders to deal with disruptors is to start a new firm with its own cost and management structures [4]. The new firm should aim to serve a cheap new segment below the proven one. It should compete with the upstarts. The old firm should go on in much the same way as before; its role is to keep its edge in the old market.

From one point of view, the Big Four did the right thing to stay out of the small footprint (or fast shopping) sector.

What does Christensen say about the chances that it would work for the market leaders to start a new low-price group? It seems that his findings are that it seldom works [5]. Huh? He shows why disruptors tend to keep their edge. The odds are that if any of the Big Four tried to create a new rival to the Small Two they would fail. That doesn't mean they would fail, but it might not be wise to bet the farm that they succeed.

What about tweaking?

If the Big Four can't or won't try to play catch-up, what are the chances that they can tweak their way out of trouble? Tweaking may be no more than a shortcut version of catch-up. But it may help slow down the fall in profits of the Big Four. At least until they can find how to deal with the main snag: their cost structure.

What if they also built on their strengths? Their strength versus the Small Two is their wide product range. Their strength versus online is that they can stock the kind of goods that don't sell well online. For instance, where the shopper wants to see or feel them before they buy: perishables may fit this bill.

Could the Big Four fix their cost structure and at the same time add to their wide range? That is, could they 'face the Minotaur'?

To fix their cost structure they'd need to close two gaps with the Small Two: cost of sales and running costs. Suppose they were to boost their range of store brands. And say they placed them on the shelves in such a way that, with time, the range of national brands shrank. The higher margins on these store brands would cut their cost of sales as a whole. It might also use less floor space. They'd still have to pay for the space that they saved, but they could stock it with a new range of non-grocery goods. They would want these to be goods that both the Small Two and the online shops would find hard to match.

Would the Big Four need to invade a new category? Or could they expand on one that they are in at present? It would be best to aim for one where the margins are high for those who specialise in it. Ready meals may be one such category. Fast food outlets prepare meals in real time, so they need gross margins of 50 to 75pc. Supermarkets don't need such high margins; there are firms that mass produce ready meals for them, not in real time. So from a cost point of view the Big Four could invade fast food with ease.

They could stock a huge range of ready meals. They have ample space and a large number of shoppers. They have regional centres to balance demand, and quick transport to the stores. Their IT systems can give real-time sales data for each type of dish. It might take up too much space for Small Two stores to match such a wide range of meals.

These may seem to be small measures, and slow to implement. But it's hard to find and keep an edge in the supermarket sector.

How might it work in the Case Study? By how much could Mastt close the cost gap with Illiad? Or we could rephrase the question. How much would the cost gap need to be in order to balance Mastt's wide range against Illiad's low prices? Suppose the cost gap is now 25pc, being 17pc cost of sales and 8pc fixed costs (per Topic 44). Suppose that store brands are now half of sales and that Mastt bumped them up by half again. That would halve the cost of sales gap. Suppose that they could close the fixed costs gap by a fifth. The total gap would now drop from 25pc to 15pc. By how much might that slow the migration of why-pay-more shoppers to Illiad?

At a 15pc gap, a household that spends £60 a week with Illiad could switch to Mastt and spend £70. Some Mastt shoppers might be glad to pay £10 more for the convenience of choosing from its wide range. They would not migrate to Illiad. At the end of the day there are bound to be fewer why-pay-more shoppers at a gap of 15pc than 25pc.

Some of this thinking about Mastt may apply to the Big Four. Each of the Big Four should aim to match – not beat – the prices of the other three groups, to avoid a futile price war. They should have the clear aim to cut their fixed costs at a faster rate than their fall in market share.

This book is just about the wars, not how to resolve them [6]. The reader may want to think about what would be the best thing for the leaders to do. Or to just keep an eye on what they in fact do.

Update: March 2017
There seems to have been a sharp surge in the range of ready meals in some of the Big Four stores, and of store brands. The first may be seen as a threat by the takeaway food sector. The second may be seen as a threat by the giant FMCG firms.

TOPIC 57 NOTES

[1] 'How big a threat...': the bulletin below compares retail sales in August 2016 with August 2015. We can't say that future growth will be like that of the past; but it can act as a guide for further study. My figures are

rough and rounded.

All retail sales went up by 4.1pc (see: 'Table 2: Sector summary'). Of that, online retail sales went up by 18.5pc, from 12.5pc, that is, from an eighth of all retail sales, to 14.3pc, or a seventh of all retail sales (see: '6. Internet sales in detail').

Now, online retail sales went up more or less 14.4pc faster than all retail sales (18.5pc minus 4.1pc). At this rate of growth, by 2020, online retail sales would be 24.5pc, or close to a quarter of all retail sales. We can cross-check this: to go from 12.5pc to 14.3pc in one year is a growth rate of 14.4pc.

On the other hand, the prospect for online food retail sales is less bullish than for all online retail sales. Online food retail sales are just 4.7pc – that's less than a twentieth – of all food retail sales (vs. 14.3pc). And they went up by 10.3 pc (see: 'Table 4: Summary of internet statistics, August 2016'). This is more or less 6.2pc faster than all retail sales went up (10.3pc minus 4.1pc). At this rate of growth, by 2020, online food retail sales would be 6pc, or one seventeenth of all food retail sales.

Once more, these are rough figures. For instance, online retail sales are a part of all retail sales; we would need to split these before we work out a net growth rate. I have made a few such approximations. All the same, they may cause no more than rounding errors.

This is the bulletin: ons.gov. uk/ business industry and trade/ retail industry/ bulletins/ retail sales/ aug2016 # main-figures. See also retail research. org/ online retailing. php. And for '(Up) to a third of all retail sales ...' see Chris Rhodes, 'The retail industry: statistics and policy' (House of Commons Library, Briefing Paper, Number 06186, 2 October 2015): he writes that online sales may be 34% by 2020; and that there will be 31% fewer stores in town centres.

[2] See Max Roser's our world in data. org/ gdp-growth-over-the-last-centuries. See also Matt Ridley, 'The Rational Optimist' (London: Fourth Estate, 2010/ 2011), 217-235.

[3] See also weforum. org/ agenda/ 2015/ 11/ most-influential-business-thinker

[4] Clayton M Christensen, 'The Innovator's Dilemma' (New York: Harper Business, 1997/2003).

[5] As per Note [4] above. See also Clayton M Christensen and M Raynor, 'The Innovator's Solution' (Boston: Harvard Business School Press, 2003) for more detail on what a disruptor should do. See also retail research. org/ whose gone bust. php for two recent instances where food retail firms have parted from groups that they once owned.

[6] Alastair Dryburgh gives a succinct summary of some of the issues: see management today.co. uk/ why-tesco-cant-compete-aldi-lidl/ future-business/ article/ 1317297: last updated 21 April 2015

Topic 58: Cramming

HOW CAN ONE tell if throughput at a store is too low? The snag could be too little supply or too little demand. It's easy to tell which is which.

In the first case, there is a bottleneck at the checkout. There are too many shoppers in the queues. The risk is that the store may lose not just sales, but also shoppers who never come back. It's hard to measure this kind of loss. Here the snag is that supply is less than demand.

They could solve it if they added checkouts (space), or if they sped up the process of checking out (time). Either way, the end result would be the same: more people would go through the checkouts in the same amount of time.

In the second case, too few shoppers go through the checkout. There aren't enough shoppers in the store. These are not real costs, just lost chances to make profit. It's also hard to measure this kind of loss. Here the snag is that demand is less than supply.

The store partly solves this in the short term if they stretch or shrink staff numbers at short notice. They need to manage their rotas, and choose in real-time when to close or open the next checkout. This lets them change some of their fixed costs (wages) into variable costs. In the long term they could change the size of the store.

In both types of snag, throughput is too low. The symptom is that supply and demand are out of kilter. Could there be one root cause? If so, could they get rid of both snags with one solution?

A small store that has no fast shopping is just a small store. The Small Two stretched the capacity of each small store at no cost by using fast shopping. It has given them more control over their supply than the Big Four.

A store might control its supply but can it control its demand? There are big swings in demand at each store throughout the day. If demand is too high shoppers might leave, or stay under pressure. If demand is too low it seems such a waste of good space.

What if most of their shoppers are regulars? How could the store control their shopping habits? Might it not be a case of right shopper, wrong time? Is there a way to get some shoppers who shop when a store is full to shop when it's empty? This would open up some more space at peak times for new shoppers.

Could they persuade some of those who shop with them at peak times to shop with them at trough times? They may find peak-time shoppers from their loyalty card system. Would it work to give them a happy hour discount if they shop in trough times? Off their total bill?

Stores' gross margin (per cent) would go down. For a net gain, gross profit in GBP would have to go up by more than the loss. Store groups would have the data to compare a large number of stores, and the ebb and flow of demand over time. From that they might work out the best times to have happy hours.

It may be too much of a risk for a leader to try happy hour pricing; their main problem is how to shrink their floor space. And it might not bring in any new shoppers – it might just change the times at which some of their regulars shop. Yet there may be too much idle space to ignore the problem. It may be worthwhile for a small group to take on the risk. Perhaps if they are short of space and want to cram more sales into the space that they have to pay for. It would need a cramming mind-set [1]. The internet has shown us that when it comes to floor space we might find that one of these days all retailers will need to have a cramming mind-set.

When marketers are knee-high they learn the three golden rules of retail. Location. But those rules no longer apply. Many types of goods (and services) can now be bought online. Location seems to be left out of the frame. What is the new golden rule? Why is this not yet clear to us all? The reason is that online has taken a while to reach the tipping point. It grew from a small base: from zero. Now it's well over 10pc of retail. So the impact of the change will soon be clear for all to see.

But we still like to buy groceries in person. Even if it costs us up to 22pc more than online – which is how much grocers pay in running costs for their stores. It would pay the grocers to bring those costs down a bit. There may still be time.

TOPIC 58 NOTES

[1] See trend watching. com/ trends/ pdf/ 2014-02%20 CRAMMING% 20 AP. pdf

Topic 59: Scoreboard: recap

MOST PEOPLE SHOP for groceries at least once a week. But they don't care what goes on behind the scenes, unless they can make some cash from it or save time.

Yet no one is better placed to judge what's going on than the shopper. They are in the stores so often that they can see with their own eyes. In this book I've described how I think it works.

In the last few years the Big Four have lost market share to the Small Two. Experts have come up with a list of outside causes of this big change. But what they say is like the tip of the iceberg: the rest is much more dramatic. Most causes came not just from the outside, but from choices made on the inside in the past 'on purpose'.

To start with, I trawled quite a few sources to come up with a list of outside causes. They all cropped up more than once, so there was no need to quote any one of them. Readers may wish to change my star ratings, which are subjective.

1. Shoppers prefer small local stores to big ones out of town. (5*)
2. Shoppers like to shop a few times a week, not just once. (5*)
3. Shoppers have had less cash since the 2008 banking crash. (5*)
4. Shoppers have spent less since their real incomes fell. (5*)
5. Shoppers prefer to shop online. (5*)

6. Shoppers lost trust in the store groups after the meat scandal. (0*)
7. Price wars between Big Four stores led to cash problems. (0*)
8. There might have been fraud inside some firms. (0*)
9. Some stores bully their suppliers. (0*)
10. The Big Four are too large and don't try hard enough. (0*)

TOTAL: 25-stars

In the history of medicine, the cure has been known to be as bad as the disease. Or it brought on what it was trying to prevent. Take the practice of bloodletting [1]. It was a common remedy up to two hundred years ago. Up to then it had been well thought of by doctors. Yet some said that it was the main cause of death. Others said it made people too weak to fight the illness it was meant to cure.

Why did our forebears do this for thousands of years? The methods of science as we know it were invented during the 1600s, yet the bleeding carried on for at least two hundred years after that.

Doctors who believed in it might have spent years tending patients. Some of these doctors might have felt that it could not be a useless and dangerous practice or else their careers would have been a waste.

Patients might have felt heady from the loss of blood. Or they took it to be a sign of their triumph over the forces of nature. They might have thought their feeling of being washed out was proof that they had got rid of frightful toxins.

But from what we now know, it seems that all they did was to physically drain their bodies.

It may be true that it's fast shopping and the small footprint of Small Two stores that lets them charge such low prices. If so, then for the Big Four to take them on in a deep price war is akin to bloodletting. All it does is drain their cash reserves. It will persist until they grasp this fact and start to deal with the main challenge.

It may be fine in the short term for the Big Four to compete on price with their close rivals. But, at the same time, they should each work on a new strategy to deal with the long-term threat from the Small Two.

In this next list I state why I think the Small Two are ahead and why they'll stay ahead. None of the items came about from outside causes. All came about from choices made on purpose over many years. Once again my star rating is subjective.

1. Shoppers can pay up to a third less for goods of the same quality. (15*)
2. Shoppers can do most of their shopping in two thirds of the time. (15*)
3. Shoppers like their grocery shopping to be quick and cheap. (10*)
4. Shoppers prefer the peace of mind of EDLP to bogofs/ offers. (5*)
5. Owner-run firms can reinvest their profits to grow faster. (5*)
6. No outside shareholders to coerce them to make quick profits. (5*)
7. It's hard for the Big Four to grow their store-

brand range. (5*)
8. It's hard for the Big Four to cut fixed costs. (5*)
9. It's hard for the Big Four to narrow scope. (5*)
10. It's hard for the Big Four to move their big stores close to town. (5*)

TOTAL: 75-stars

I set out below a few remarks to expand on some of the points above. In the main they are to do with why the Small Two are able to charge so much less than the rest. The points are linked and they overlap.

- High-margin store brands enable lower prices.
- Fast throughput enables lower margins/prices.
- Fast throughput is made possible by small stores, less choice, and fast checkouts.
- Small stores are made possible by fewer products, a smaller range, and narrow aisles.
- Small stores mean lower running costs.
- The Big Four are locked into ways of doing things that make it hard for them to respond.

Star ratings for the two lists add up to 100, so we may as well call them 'percentages'. If we combine the lists and put the fifteen items in sequence we could call this new list 'reasons that the Small Two are winning the supermarket wars'.

TOPIC 59 NOTES

[1] See: today.duke. edu/ 2000/ 02/ blood218

Topic 60: Update: coverage

LATE IN 2016 I read in a news item in a broadsheet that Lidl's growth had peaked, sales per store were falling, and its rivals were fighting back.

This opens up a whole new vista to explore.

We can use the term 'coverage' to mean how widely stores are spread in the UK. Over the years, Lidl would have grown in one region at a time. As a region filled up with stores they would land up being closer to each other. Lidl would not want them to be so close that they would poach each other's shoppers.

But it's clear that the denser their coverage the closer their stores will be to each other. If they are too close then at some point sales in each store might even fall. This would be where both stores have to share the pool of shoppers. The issue is 'how close is too close?'

Lidl will have defined their aims in terms of numbers. For instance, they might want 'nine out of ten shoppers to be within twenty minutes of a Lidl.' And they might want 'Lidl stores to be no closer than fifteen minutes apart.' In each region, once they come close to these numbers they might move to the next region.

My guess has been that poaching between their own stores will not be a snag prior to the Small Two reaching 20pc market share. They should reach 20pc once they have 2000 stores. This should be in about 2020.

How can we test the three claims put forward at the start of this topic? What is the evidence that Lidl's growth has peaked, that its sales per store are falling, and that its rivals are fighting back?

We can best start with the second item. The press release does not say why Lidl's sales per store might be falling. They say it may have passed the 'peak of its potency' but don't explain what this means or why. I have tried to guess why they think Lidl sales per store might be falling.

One way sales could fall is if coverage in the UK by Lidl is so dense that its stores poach from each other. We don't know what the real numbers are so we have to look for clues.

Lidl have said they plan to double their store count in the UK in the next few years [1]. Aldi has also said they plan to double their store count. Let's say they aren't bluffing. That means they don't think coverage will be too dense.

But we need some facts to support this.

In 2015, Tesco had more than 700 large stores with a mean area of more than 2700 sq. m. each. They also had close to 200 metro stores with a mean area of more than 1000 sq. m. each [2].

Sainsbury's had some 600 large stores with a mean area of more than 3000 sq. m. each [3].

For both of these groups one would presume that their store count would give them enough coverage, yet without it being too dense. Their stores would be fairly spread.

It strikes me that the coverage of both Lidl and Aldi is sparse compared to these two rivals. Lidl and Aldi stores are much less than 1500 sq. m. [4]. This means there should be ample room for up to 1000 stores from each group, with no fear of poaching within each group.

So if Lidl's sales per store are falling it's not for this reason.

It's clear that there will be more and more stores from rival groups competing toe-to-toe close to where we shoppers shop. That's the whole aim. The Small Two don't mind a slugging match based on price; they want why-pay-more shoppers from their rivals to migrate their way.

The next step is to find facts to check the other claims at the start of this topic. We can first use the stunning graphic on the Kantar Worldpanel site [5] to see how my guesses are panning out. The three dates are September 2014, 2015, 2016.

The market share for the Big Four went from 73pc to 72pc to 70pc: my guess was 61pc by 2020. The trend is going the right way but not yet as fast as I thought.

The share for the rest went from 18pc to 19pc to 19pc: my guess was that it would stay the same. So far that's close enough.

The share for the Small Two went from 8pc to 10pc to 11pc: my guess was 20pc by 2020. The rate of gain is slowing down but there is plenty of time for it to catch up. The Small Two feel no pain when they price low. But if the Big Four keep on with their discounts they may run out of ammo – which, in this case, is cash. Then the Small Two's rate of gain should speed up again.

We can look at the graphic one month on, to October 2016. There is almost no real change, except the Big Four's market share went up by a tenth of one per cent. Are the claims (above) all based on this one month? Do they see it as a portent that the 'German discounters' are running out of steam? Despite the trend of the last two years?

Does it mean they think that the change in the last two years has been just a big wave? When all the time it has been the new tide coming in?

Tides also count

If one hasn't done a Little analysis it may be hard to detect the new tide. This tide – fueled by the internet – may sweep through the rest of retail in the next few years. To know how to use flow rate won't keep it at bay. But it may help to prepare some defence.

There might be a few reasons for sales in one store group to slow down for a short time. Say it takes six months for a new store to break even. If a store group has a spate of new store openings they could have dozens of stores where sales are not yet up to speed. This could bring down the mean sales for the group for a short time.

Having said all this, does it matter if the mean sales per Lidl store slows down or halts in the next few years? Nope. The 20pc target doesn't depend on mean sales per store going up. It depends on the store count. What happens if the mean sales per store stay the same but there are twice as many stores as in 2014? Total sales in GBP will be twice what they were in 2014 (see Topic 4). On its own that will take the Small Two close to 20pc market share.

There seems to be no good reason to think that the sales per store of new Small Two stores will be less than they are now.

It's also best not to cling too tightly to the numbers from just one month (October 2016). It's best to look at them over time and keep asking 'why'.

Christensen says of the low-end disruptors that they find a way to keep their fixed costs lower than their rivals. It is how they can afford to have lower gross margins [7]. Porter says that the basic aim of a generic strategy is to find an edge; and that the supreme aim is to keep it [8]. The Small Two found a way to keep their edge – 'keep it small and speed it up' – in a way that rivals can't match. It's why their fixed costs are lower than their rivals; which in turn is why they can afford to have lower gross margins; which is why they can sell goods for less; and, finally, which is why the why-pay-more shoppers migrate their way.

The problem could be ignored in the past. The Small Two did not have much market share. There is a point where size starts to matter. For instance, say a disruptor firm starts with a 1pc share of a static market. Its share goes up by 50pc each year. At that rate, in five years it will have a 7.5pc share. Its rivals might feel they can live with that. Perhaps. But say a disruptor firm starts with a 10pc share of a static market. Its share goes up by 50pc each year. At that rate, in five years it will have a 75pc share. By then most of its rivals will have left the market.

There may be a few learning points here. Watch the growth rate of your rivals and don't assume it will slow down. Don't rely on a snapshot, but keep tabs on it over time. Look at the starting-point as well as the trajectory.

We can just wait until 2020 to see the results.

TOPIC 60 NOTES

[1]telegraph.co. uk/ finance/ news by sector/ retail and consumer/ 10486418/ Lidl-plans-to-more-than-double-number-of-stores-in-UK
[2] en.wikipedia. org/ wiki/ Tesco# UK_operations
[3] en.wikipedia. org/ wiki/ Sainsbury%27s # Stores
[4] mirror.co. uk/ money/ lidl-set-open-50-shops-6813235
[5] See.kantar world panel. com/ en/ grocery-market-share/ great-britain/ snapshot / 09.10.16
[6] See this item from early 2016: news.sky. com/ story/ tesco-to-axe-thousands-of-head-office-jobs-10373497
[7] Clayton M Christensen and M Raynor, 'The Innovator's Solution' (Boston: Harvard Business School Press, 2003), 50.
[8] See Topic 30, Note [2]: hbr. org/ 1986/ 09/ sustainable-advantage

Acknowledgements

BY FAR THE best teachers that I ever had were Bob Boland, Meyer Feldberg and Phil Riese, and the UCT MBA Class of '72 who brought it all to life.

After business school I found only one learning system to rival the Harvard Business School Case Study method. That came from working with clients to solve real life business problems. This phase lasted for the rest of my time in consulting.

I don't think I would have started writing had I not read Rudolf Flesch; and were it not for the thousands of people who built Microsoft Word and Amazon. Flesch's books taught me that there is virtue in trying to write in plain words. MS Word is much better than the advanced typewriters that I once used to write business reports; and its Flesch reading stats have turned out to be indispensable. Finally, with Amazon, I can write and publish with no fuss.

I was lucky to be able to spend years exploring ideas that interested me, simply because they were valued by clients. I hope the same will apply to ideas that I present to readers. For those who enjoyed this book, I would be obliged if you would be so kind as to tell your friends; and, if you use social media, to tell your connections. Ask them to find this book by keying its main title into the Search box on the Amazon website (that helps my book's rankings). They can use the "Look Inside" feature as their free sample. And, if you have the time, I would be much obliged if you would write a review (on Amazon); kindly mention the three to five topics you liked the most, such as T11, T28, T47, T52. Please use the reference UKSW 1.1 for this edition. Thanks!

About the author

G. N. C. PARKER WRITES BUSINESS books for ordinary people. After getting an MBA at UCT he spent over twenty years as a consultant to business owners. During that time he also founded and ran a national training firm for business owners and managers. He also wrote and rented out business software long before 'the cloud'.

In between he spent five years in sales. He was a rep at IBM for a year, where he sold mainframe systems; and he was an investment property broker for four years.

He took time out for two years to teach core MBA subjects at Wits Business School.

He has two degrees from distance learning – BA, with majors in economics and psychology, and BSc (Hons) in computing – and an ACII.

He and his wife live in Norfolk, England.

Index

Names

Refers to Topic number; access via Table of Contents ('n' means Notes)

Ackoff, Russell 37n; Anderson, Chris 46n; Anthony, Robert 6n; Bauer, Andras 37n; Bezos, Jeff 37n; Buckingham, Marcus 43n; Cachon, Gerard 3n, 39n; Champy, James 39n; Christensen, Clayton 31, 31n, 53, 53n, 57, 57n, 60, 60n; Coffman, Curt 43n; Dell, Michael 42n; Dennett, Daniel C 8n; Dickens, Charles 3, 3n; Drucker, Peter 11, 11n, 20n, 28, 28n; Dryburgh, Alistair 57n; Fisher, Roger 45n; Franz, Josep 37n; Gamma, Erich 12n; Garner, Ed 11n; Gigerenzer, Gerd 37n; Hammer, Michael 39n; Handy, Charles 15n; Hanrahan, Jack 7n, 12n; Hawkins, David 6n; Helm, Richard 12n; Jobs, Steve 37n; Johnson, Ralph 12n; Jones, Owen 15n; Kahneman, Dan 37n; Maestripieri, Dario 31n; Marx, Chico 3; Meise, Jan Niklas 37n; Merchant, Kenneth A 6n; Morelli, Carlo 11n; Pearce, Michael 12n; Peppers, Don 16n; Pinker, Steven 32n; Polya G 28n; Porter, Michael, 29, 29n, 57, 60; Raynor, M 57n, 60n; Rhodes, Chris 57n; Ridley, Matt 57n; Rogers, Martha 16n; Roosevelt, Teddy 53n; Roser, Max 57n; Rudolph, Thomas 37; Schilit, Howard 49n; Schlegelmilch, Bodo B 37n; Schlesinger, Joseph 12n; Schumpeter, Joseph 31, 31n; Simon, Herbert A 37n; Stevenson, Laurence 12n; Sunstein, Cass R 40n; Terwiesch, Christian 3n, 39n; Thaler, Richard H 40n; Ury, William 45n; Vlissides, John 12n; Walters, David 7n, 12n

Subjects

Refers to Topic number; access via Table of Contents ('n' means Notes)

90s – see 'nineties'

acting on purpose 2, 7-9, 53, 59

advertising 4, 50, 55; above-the-line- 16; below-the-line- 16

Agency problem 48

Aladdin's Cave effect 12, 17

Aldi 1, 4, 4n, 9-10, 13n, 47, 51, 57n, 60

AMD 53, 53n

Asda 1, 10

assumptions 4, 35-6

balance sheet 2, 6, 20-1, 39, 52

banking crash 2008: 4, 7, 8, 11, 32, 52, 59

best-of-both: range and price 12; downside and upside 35; long lease with options 54

big bang approach 55-6

Big Four 1-2, 4-5, 7-10, 12-13, 21, 24-5, 27-32, 34, 47, 51-4, 56-60

bloodletting 59

bobbing corks 7, 8, 53

bogof (and HLP) 6, 8, 12, 14, 16, 17, 17n, 47, 47n, 59

bookies 6, 49

bottlenecks 2, 8, 8n, 34, 36, 58

bottom-up/ bubble up 33, 37

brand: -image 16; -loyalty 16

break even 35, 52, 60

bullies – see 'shirkers'

business: -model 28, 53; -owner 2, 48

buyer 45

capacity 3, 4, 36, 38, 40, 47, 51, 53, 58

Case Study – see 'Illiad Case Study'

cashier 37, 43

Category management (CM) 11, 17, 23, 44, 45, 57

CEO 42n, 49-50, 54

checkout 2, 8-9, 14, 36-8, 40-1, 43, 58-9

Companies Act 48

competitive advantage – see 'edge'

computer 32, 37, 45

consultant 3, 9, 39

contribution 27; -margin 27n

convenience: 12, 14, 38, 57; -store 12, 32

Co-op 10

Cost: -of sales 5, 6, 11, 21-24, 26-27, 44, 47, 52, 57; -structure 1, 7, 21-23, 25, 32, 34-5, 41, 52, 57; cost-plus 22

costs: asset- 4; fixed- 7-8, 14, 17, 26-27, 35, 38, 40-1, 44, 47, 49, 52-3, 55, 57-60; holding- 11, 39; labour- 26, 34; non-operating- 6, 21; operating- 52 (see costs: running); other variable- 27; running- 3-6, 12, 21-23, 26, 27, 34-5, 38, 46, 53-4, 57, 59; unit- 8; variable- 14, 27, 35, 52, 58

coverage 60

creative destruction 31

cross-train 27, 37

culture of the firm 43-4

customer 3, 11, 16, 20, 30-2, 37n, 43, 45, 47-8, 53, 54n

debt 2, 20, 35, 42, 49, 52

demand 3n, 11, 20, 32-3, 35, 39n, 42, 46n, 48-9, 51, 54, 57-8

demographics 15, 15n

discount 5, 11, 12, 14, 20, 23-7, 34-5, 38, 44-5, 49, 55, 58, 60; discounted (present value) 54

discounter 4, 11, 13, 15, 44; German- 4, 7, 60; hard- 13

discovery 19, 19n

disruptive innovation 2, 15, 31-2, 31n, 46, 53, 55, 57, 60

dividends 13, 20, 42, 49

economies: of scale 16-17, 16n; of scope 16, 16n

edge, an 11, 17, 18, 30, 39, 46, 47, 49, 57, 60

EDLP 6, 12, 14-17, 29, 44, 47, 57, 59

effective 12, 28

efficient 12, 28, 35, 49n, 38

equity 20

evolution 31

fast shopping 1-2, 4-5, 8, 14-15, 18, 32, 34-6, 38-40, 47, 51, 55, 57-60

financial: -engineering 49, 49n, 54; -gearing 49, 52; -judgement 49, 51; -policy 20; -risk 49, 51-2; -statements 2, 6n, 27

fixed assets 21, 34, 39, 49, 52

flow rate 2-4, 8, 28, 35-6, 38-41, 58-60

FMCG 6, 11, 44, 47

founder 9, 42n, 48

framework 2, 28, 31-2; see also 'model'

free: -market 31; -riders – see 'shirkers'

fund manager 13, 49

GDP 6, 57n

gearing 2, 49, 52-4

groceries 7, 11, 12, 14-19, 23, 28-30, 37-8, 45, 47, 52-3, 56-7, 59; basic- 4, 11, 14, 16, 29-30, 53, 56-7; -sector 10, 52

gross profit – see 'profit'

guess/ prediction 1, 2, 4, 8, 25, 27, 44, 49-50, 54, 60

halo effect 45, 45n

HLP – see 'bogof'

Homer Glass 9, 15-19, 33, 37-46, 49-50, 55

house brand – see 'store brand'

household 3, 10, 10n, 56-7; -name 14, 44

IBM 31-2

IESE Business School 13, 13n

Illiad 2, 9, 13-20, 25, 33-46, 49, 50, 55, 57; Case Study 1, 2, 9, 13-19, 33-4, 37-46, 49-50, 55, 57; Illiad Case

Study 9, 15-19, 33, 37-40, 42-6, 49-50, 55
Illy 9, 15-19, 33, 37-46, 49-50, 55
impulse (buy) 12, 14, 18-19, 37, 46
industry-wide 29, 47
inflation 1, 10, 10n, 11
Intel 53, 53n
internet 2-3, 7, 18-19, 22, 27, 37, 39, 46, 53, 57n, 58, 60
investor 49, 54
IP 6, 44
IT 6, 11-12, 16, 30, 33-4, 39, 46, 57
jobs 3, 37, 37n, 43, 56, 60n
Johnny: -British 15; -Foreigner 15, 55
Kantar Worldpanel 10, 11n, 60
keep it small and speed it up 1, 4-5, 34-6, 39, 51, 55, 57,
      59-60
leaseback 2, 54
leverage – see 'gearing'
Lidl 1, 4, 4n, 9-10, 47, 51, 57n, 60, 60n
Little's Law 2, 15, 28, 38n, 39, 60
long tail 14, 46, 46n
long-term/ long term 1, 7, 15-16, 20, 33, 42, 49, 53-4,
      57-59
low-cost leader 14-15, 29-30, 47, 57
luxury goods 12, 15-17, 46
mainframe 31-2
management accounts 27
managers 7, 9, 13, 20, 27, 30, 33, 37-8, 43, 48-9, 52
margin: gross- 2, 4, 9, 12, 14, 17, 20-5, 27, 34, 38, 44-5,
      47, 52-3, 58, 60; operating- 21, 23, 34, 44
market: UK grocery- 31; free- 31; -fragmentation 53; -
      leaders 9, 25, 52, 57; -orientated 16; -price 54; -
      rent 54; -share 1, 4, 9, 10-11, 25-6, 28, 30, 59-60;
      -size 4, 10; -structure 7
marketing 12, 14, 15n, 16n, 28, 32, 37
mark-up 22
Mastt 2, 9, 13-20, 23-6, 34-41, 44-46, 49-50, 52, 55, 57

mission: shopping- 12; -statement 33

model 2, 8, 9, 12, 13, 18, 28, 36, 53, 55; see also 'framework'

modular/ modules 12, 45

Morrison's 1, 10

national brand 4, 5, 12, 14, 26, 44-45, 47, 57

negotiate/ negotiator 45, 54

nineties 2, 11, 12, 14, 18, 28, 30-1, 39, 52

non-groceries 12, 14, 37, 52, 57

nudge 14, 40, 40n, 44

one-stop shop 12, 14, 17, 46, 51

one-to-one 11, 16, 16n, 39

online 2, 3, 9, 19, 39, 44, 51, 52, 55, 57, 57n, 59

operating profit – see 'profit, operating (OP)'

ops mgmt./ operations management 3n, 6, 11, 28, 39n

own brand – see 'store brand'

owner-run (private company/ firm) 6, 9, 13, 15, 48-50, 54, 59

parking 2, 12, 14, 36, 38, 40

peak times 3-5, 14, 34-5, 37-8, 40, 58

peer pressure/ rivalry 43

pile 'em high 5, 11, 15, 34, 39

plan 4, 11-12, 15, 18, 20, 33, 34n, 45, 47, 49-51, 60, 60n

plc/ public (limited) company 6, 9, 13, 15, 48-50, 54

pound stores 27

prediction – see 'guess'

present value 54

price: -fixing 13; market- 51, 54; -point 14; selling- 22, 24, 44, 53; share- 13, 21, 49, 54; -signalling 12; -tags 37;- war 4, 13, 25, 57, 59

primary shoppers/ choice 12, 15, 48

private company/ firm – see 'owner-run'

private label – see 'store brand'

product line – see 'SKU'

product: -award 15; -line 14, 35; -mix 12, 16; -orientated 16; -range 2, 5, 8, 12-14, 16, 29-30, 37, 40-1, 44-

46, 55, 57, 59; -recipe 44-5; -scope 46; -specs 44-45

profit 22; gross- (GP) 6, 21-7, 34-5, 38-40, 44-5, 52; net- 6, 21, 52, 54; operating- (OP) 4, 6, 21, 23, 25-7, 34-6, 38, 40, 52-3; -plough back 13, 49, 59; -windfall 54; -before interest and tax (PBIT) 6, 21

profit and loss account 2, 6, 20-1, 39, 52

property 2, 6, 21, 51, 53-4, 54n

public company – see 'plc'

public sector – see 'sector, state'

punters 15, 15n, 49

queue 36-7, 44, 58

ready/ pre-made meals 15, 18, 57

region 33, 45, 55, 57, 60

rent 3-4, 6, 8, 10, 12, 14, 17, 21, 23, 26, 28, 30, 32, 34, 37-41, 47, 51-5, 57; net- 54

return on investment 20, 39

revolution 31, 39n

risk 1, 2, 11, 14, 16-17, 26, 32, 35, 40, 44-45, 47-9, 51-4, 57-8; -averse 35, 49

Royal Society 3

rules of thumb 2, 23, 28, 33, 37, 52-54

safety margin 53

Sainsbury's 1, 10, 17n, 47n, 60, 60n

sale and leaseback 2, 54

sales 1, 3, 4n, 4-8, 10-11, 14, 18-19, 21-7, 30, 32, 34-5, 37-40, 44-8, 51-5, 57-8, 60; -growth 4, 51-2, 55; -per sq. m 1, 4, 11, 35, 54; -per store 1, 35, 60; -per year 1; -per hour 5, 38

scale up 32

scan rate 37

scope 2, 9, 14, 16, 16n, 29-30, 37, 46-7, 53, 57, 59

sector 2, 3, 3n, 12, 23, 32, 39, 47-8, 48n, 51-3, 57n; gro-cery/ supermarket- 1, 2-4, 4n, 7, 9, 10, 11n, 12, 14, 22, 25, 28, 30-2, 34-5, 47-53, 51n, 55-57, 60n;

manufacturing- 48; primary- 48; private- 48; public- – see 'state sector'; secondary- 48; services- 48; state- 48, 56; tertiary- 48;

segment 29-31, 47, 53, 57

services firm 2, 39, 48-9

shareholder 7, 9, 13, 15, 20, 42, 48-9, 54, 59

shares 6

shirkers/ bullies/ free riders 33, 43

shopping: -basket-size 12, 14, 46, 55; -convenience 12, 14; -experience 12, 14, 17, 37; -habits 7, 14, 58; -mission 12, 15; -mood 12, 17-18, 46; one-stop- 12, 46; -process 2, 9, 14-15, 19, 34, 46, 56; -speed/ fast- 2, 4-5, 8, 14-15, 18-19, 28, 32, 34-40, 46, 51, 55, 57-9

SKU 6, 11-12, 14, 37, 46

slice – see 'segment'

small footprint and fast shopping 2, 4-5, 8, 12, 14-15, 18, 30, 32, 34-5, 40, 51, 53, 55, 57-9

Small Two 1-2, 4-5, 7-10, 11n, 13, 25, 27-32, 34-6, 47, 52-3, 57-60

staff -incentives 33, 37, 43; -turnover 43, 56

standard/s 6, 8, 14-15, 17, 19, 31, 33, 36-7, 43-5, 55, 57

stealth -mode/ -tactics 2, 9, 15, 49-50, 55

stock 2, 4, 6, 11, 11n, 12, 14-19, 21, 27, 33-4, 37-9, 44-8, 48n, 55, 57

store: -brand 2-6, 11-12, 14, 26, 37, 41, 44-5, 47, 55, 57, 59; -count 4, 50, 52, 55, 60; -format 37; -size 2, 4, 8, 33, 41, 43, 46, 58-60; -count 4, 50, 52, 55, 60

strategy 7, 7n, 8, 11, 11n, 12, 12n, 17, 20, 26, 28-29, 29n, 30-1, 39, 50, 52-4, 56n, 59-60

structure: 1, 7, 7n, 11, 11n, 12, 18, 21-3, 25, 27-8, 32-5, 41, 43, 52, 57; cost- 1, 7, 21-3, 25, 32, 34-35, 41, 52, 57

supplier 1, 3, 5, 6, 8-9, 11, 13, 15, 17, 19, 21, 26, 37-8, 43-4, 44n, 45, 47, 59

supply 3, 3n, 11, 11n, 20, 22, 32-3, 39, 39n, 44-5, 51, 58;
    -chain 11, 39, 45
supermarket 1-4, 4n, 7, 9, 11-12, 17n, 18, 22-3, 29-30,
    34, 34n, 43-4, 44n, 45n, 46, 47n, 51n, 52n, 54n,
    56-7, 59
sustainable competitive advantage – see 'edge'
target market 12, 29-30, 32, 46
team 18, 33, 37, 43, 45, 47
Tesco 1, 4n, 10, 32n, 52n, 57n, 60, 60n (2)
throughput – see 'flow rate'
top-down 37
trust 11, 15, 16-17, 44, 47-8, 59
value 3, 12, 14-17, 21, 36, 44, 46-9, 51, 54-5
wages 4, 8, 11, 14, 21, 23, 27, 34, 41, 47, 52, 56, 58
Waitrose 10
work backwards 8, 22, 25, 37, 37n
yield (on property) 54

Websites

Refers to Topic number; for website address, go to topic via Table of Contents ('n' means Notes)

accountingtools. com: Margin of safety 53n; marginal cost 47n; operating leverage 52n

colliers. com: Property surveys 54n

coursera. org: Bottlenecks 8n; flow-rate 8n; Little's Law 38n; ops mgmt. 3n

dailymail.co. uk: Bogofs axed 17n, 48n

economic.gouv. fr: Food retailing in Germany vs UK 13n

economist. com: Disruptive technology/ innovation 31n; family firms 48n

ey. com: Financial statements per FRS 102: 6n

fooddeserts. org: Store growth in 20 years 4n; UK grocery sales growth 51n

forbes. com: Intel and AMD 53n (2); store brand secrets 44n

ft. com: Listed PLCs 48n

getbrandwise. com: Demographics 15n

gov. uk: Part-time staff, 56n; shopper preferences 15n; statistics 2015: 48n

greece.mrdonn. org: Minotaur 53n

hbr. org: Competitor advantage 30n, 60n

hbs. edu: Christensen profile 31n

hrgrapevine. com: Staff turnover rates 56n

ieseinsight. com: Aldi 13n; hard discounters 13n

ifm.eng.cam.ac. uk: Generic strategies 29n

imdb. com: Quote by C. Marx 3n

international supermarket news. com: Aldi store openings 4n; complaints 45n

kantar world panel. com: Market shares 2016: 60n; market shares at start date 10n

management today.co. uk: Why they can't compete with

the discounters 57n
marketoracle.co. uk: Michael Dell interview 42n
mashable. com: Browsing/ discovery 19n
mirror.co. uk: Lidl to open more stores 54n
news.sky. com: Tesco to reduce jobs 60n
notablequotes. com: From Bertrand Russell 47n
nytimes. co: Skin in the game 48n
ons.gov. uk: Households 10n; employment 48n; retail industry 2016: 57n
our world in data. org: GDP growth 57n
people.cs.umass. edu: Little's Law 50 years later 39n
people.hofstra. edu: Economies of scale 16n
plma. com: Hall of fame 44n; store brands 44n
research briefings.files.parliament. uk: Labour market 48n
retail research. org: Online retail 57n; who's gone bust 57n
telegraph.co. uk: Aldi store size 4n; space race 52n; Goldman Sachs comments, 51n; Lidl to double store-count 60n
theguardian. com: Fall in fixed costs 45n
thesun.co. uk: FMCG battles 44n
thismoney.co. uk: Hidden fees 44n
thocp. net: Don Estridge biography 32n
today.duke. edu: Bloodletting 59n
trendwatching. com: Cramming 58n
uk.kantar. com: Market share update 2016: 10n
web.mit. edu: Little's Law 15n
web archive.national archives.gov. uk: Census 2011 labour market changes 48n
weforum. org: Business thinkers 57n
en.wikipedia. org: Category management 11n; competitive advantage 30n; contribution margin 27n; cost leadership 47n; creative destruction 31n; economies of scope 16n; efficient-market hypothesis 49n; five whys 8n; halo effect 45n; in-

tentional stance 8n; Joint Stock Companies Act 1856: 48n; Joseph Schumpeter 31n; Little's Law 28n, 38n; long tail 14n; marketing 16n; nullius in verba 3n; principal-agent problem 47n; Sainsbury's, stores 60n; satisficing 37n; self-serving bias 54n; structure follows strategy 7n; supply chain 11n; Tesco 32n; Tesco, UK operations 60n
wsj. com: shopping habits 54n; Dell going private 48n, 49n; UK supermarket costs 34n

Printed in Great Britain
by Amazon

54171606R00168